DEFEATING LIBERAL LIES

Books by Kenneth Tarr

Bird Legs

The Last Days Series
Gathering Storm
Pioneer One
Promised Land
End of the World

The Hive: The Best of All Possible Worlds

The Gift

Defeating Liberal Lies

DEFEATING LIBERAL LIES

At last! A book dedicated to exposing and destroying liberal tactics.

KENNETH R. TARR

Defeating Liberal Lies

Published by Truebekon Books

Ebook design by EpubMasters

ISBN: 978-0-9675174-0-7

Printed in the United States of America
Year of first electronic printing: 2020

Dedicated to all American patriots.

ACKNOWLEDGMENTS

I would like to express my gratitude to all those who made this book possible. My wife, Kathy, gave me continual moral support and patiently acted as an intelligent sounding board for all my ideas. The people at ePUBmaster did a remarkable job of creating the book. Rachel Ann Nunes edited the text and designed the cover. Catia Shattuck also edited the text and designed the print format. The ebook was designed by T. J. Nunes. And finally, hundreds of patriotic Americans inspired me by sharing their ideas and their personal experiences in the cause of fighting the growing tyranny in this country.

CONTENTS

Preface vii

Introduction x
A Brief History of the American
Experiment and Leftist Influences

Chapter One 1
The Nature and Motivation of Leftists

Chapter Two 11
The Left's Causes

Chapter Three 17
Primary Tactics of the Left: Tricky Language

Chapter Four 64
Primary Tactics of the Left: Deceptive Content

Chapter Five 117
Engaging Leftists (Rules for Debate)

Conclusion 147

Appendix A: Conservative Commentators 149

Appendix B: Conservative and Semiconservative News Sources 154

Appendix C: The Rogues' Gallery of BigLeft Organizations 159

Works Consulted 162

PREFACE

THIS BOOK EXPOSES AND REFUTES the lies and deceptive tactics of the Left. However, I need to state from the start that the Right is far from perfect. I have seen some conservatives, or people who claim to be conservatives, behave in ways that are indeed disturbing and counterproductive. Many use violent, hateful, vulgar, and abusive language. I certainly would not want to give such people the power to make laws I would have to obey.

True conservatives are relatively tolerant and objective, or at least they try to be most of the time. The problem is, however, conservatives and mainstream Americans have proved to be far too patient, far too willing to avoid conflict, far too agreeable, and far too reticent to fight back. The result has been that the Left has taken advantage of these positive qualities to discredit their opposition and to bring about the triumph of their agenda. Therefore, now is the time to fight back; now is the time to play hardball for a change.

The introduction of this book presents a brief review of the reasons for America's greatness and the Left's efforts to undermine American constitutional government and its tradition of freedom for every individual.

Chapter one deals in a general way with the nature and motivation of leftists and liberals. Chapter two lists some of the causes that liberals promote and defend. In addition to those named, the Left has a wish list that seems almost endless.

Chapter three presents many of the Left's deceptive and evasive tactics based on tricky language. Chapter four reviews some of the Left's favorite tactics founded on content.

Chapter five introduces my rules or suggestions for debating with liberals.

The book also includes three important appendices. Appendix A provides a fairly comprehensive list of conservative commentators and analysts that you can depend on for good, honest evaluations. Appendix B provides another list of dependable conservative and semi-conservative news sources. These resources will help you in debating liberals by providing you with accurate information and definitions you can trust. This is crucial because leftists love to distort meanings and use what I call Teflon definitions.

However, one problem occurs with some of these conservative news sources. In an effort to seem credible and responsible, they tend to be somewhat vacillating in their opposition to leftism. Oh, they certainly present many good arguments and factual information, but they seldom depict accurately how vicious, hateful, and devious the Left really is. They seem to be afraid to tell it like it is.

This book does not suffer from that niceness but strives instead to expose the reality of leftism. Thus, it is in essence direct, provocative, and sometimes confrontational. It shows vividly how the average leftist depends mostly on lies, duplicity, emotion, bullying, and violence. One excellent source of good definitions is Conservapedia, an online site that is constantly expanding its offerings. In this book I occasionally use definitions and information from sources like Wikipedia, but these sources often have a notoriously leftist bias, especially on controversial issues that are widely debated today. Some of these issues include global warming, gun control, immigration, vaccines, socialism versus capitalism, the legitimate role of government, political propaganda, voter ID laws, abortion, and feminism.

Appendix C provides a third list that I call the Rogues' Gallery of BigLeft Organizations. This includes the rich and the powerful, the proud and arrogant elite, the globalists and other conspirators against the freedom and happiness of all lands and nations. We must beware of them and fight them in every way possible.

Please note that in all the mini debates in this book, the participants are called "actors." The names of liberals of any stripe are followed by (L) and the conservatives by (C). The text of these debates are given exactly as they were written or verbally articulated by the actors, including all their errors in language.

INTRODUCTION

A Brief History of the American Experiment and Leftist Influences

Liberalism and progressivism, the philosophy of the Left, are a cancer that is destroying America. Progressives may smile, say nice things, claim to have good intentions, be caring, do good deeds, and even smile as they shake your hand. But their destructive beliefs lead—sooner or later—to socialism and Communism, the sociopolitical doctrines that destroy freedom, lead to economic stagnation, poverty, spiritual decline, the death of millions, and eventually to totalitarian government.

History shows that socialism and Communism produced misery, privation, and tyranny in Nazi Germany, Communist Russia, North Korea, Cambodia, Laos, Cuba, Venezuela, Argentina, and everywhere else it was practiced.

President Ronald Reagan believed that liberalism is the American version of Fascism, the blood brother of Nazism.[1]

---

1 Daily Caller News Foundation, "Liberals Hate This Reagan Video," *TheDC Shorts*, April 2, 2020, 5:36, https://www.youtube.com/watch?v=CJSZm0siRCw.

Unfortunately, even "good" people can do very bad things, sometimes without even realizing it. But is it really kind and caring to purposely or inadvertently destroy our children's future and abandon them to a life devoid of hope, deprived of freedom, and lacking the opportunities Americans have enjoyed so long? I think not, but sadly that is the path we are now on.

* * *

Good and evil have always existed on the earth from the beginning of recorded history. These two forces result from the inherent, basic nature of man, which is unchanging over time. This means that modern man has the same fundamental strengths and weaknesses as ancient man. Generally speaking, human beings are naturally inconsistent, foolish, and sinful, but they can also be self-sacrificing, kind, courageous, and charitable.

Leftists did not invent human foibles, but they typically push the negative qualities of human nature to great extremes, especially in political and social matters. One of their primary destructive mantras is to reach their goals *by any means necessary.*

By contrast, conservatives tend to seek positive goals by worthy means, and they reject the idea that the end justifies the means. Their goal is to better the world by improving the individual while the Left seeks to better the world through the power of big government.

At the beginning of the American nation, the Founding Fathers fully realized the two conflicting aspects of human nature and designed a constitution to protect the rights and freedom of the people against those who would heed their baser instincts and seek to gain power, influence, and wealth by any means necessary.

To secure the people's natural, God-given right to be free and to enjoy the fruits of their labor, the Framers wrote into the nation's supreme law—the Constitution—a unique system never before seen or practiced in the history of the world. This system is based on the separation of powers, checks and balances, and man's right to life, liberty, and property.

Their ideas were inspired by the greatest political scholars of the 18th century Enlightenment. Among those great men was John Locke, commonly known as the father of classical liberalism, who wrote *Two Treatises of Government*, and the Baron de Montesquieu, who wrote *The Spirit of the Laws.*

This balance of powers is threefold. First, in the central government, power and authority is separated into three distinct branches—the executive, the legislative, and the judicial—each with their enumerated powers and responsibilities. Thus, each branch would be hindered from usurping the enumerated powers of the other two branches. Second, Congress itself represents a balance of power between the House of Representatives and the Senate. Third, the Framers intended that the power of the federal government should be checked by the constitutional powers reserved only to the various states and the people (the Tenth Amendment).

This system of a balance of powers is called "federalism." Basically, the Constitution is designed to control the federal government, which was seen by the Framers as the most dangerous threat to the freedom of the people.

The Founding Fathers would have been astounded to see the current unconstitutional overreach exercised by the executive and judicial branches of government, while the legislative branch has largely abdicated its duties and passed them off to an unelected administrative bureaucracy. These arrogant bureaucrats claim to have good intentions, but as the saying goes "the road to hell is paved with good intentions."

Ever since the Constitution was ratified in 1788, and the United States was established as one nation, greedy and power-hungry men have striven to undermine the system and accrue power unto themselves. This movement has always existed in this nation and is not unique to modern times.

However, since the end of the 19th century and the beginning of the 20th century a movement called "classical liberalism" became prominent in Europe and later in America. In its original formulations during the Age of Enlightenment of the 18th century, liberalism was a positive political philosophy that rejected the dogmas of past oppressive regimes. But by the end of the 19th century, liberalism in Europe and America had morphed into something entirely different, something truly insidious and dangerous.

Instead of promoting freedom, tolerance, and openness, this new radical liberalism became a movement which sought by pernicious and seductive methods to control the public schools, universities, the mainstream media, the courts, the entertainment industry, Hollywood, churches, and federal and state governments. This new brand of liberals found their ideals in Marxism, Darwinism, the teachings of the German philosopher Nietzsche, and later the radical propagandist, Saul Alinsky. After learning the immense value of manipulating the meaning of words, they adopted the normally positive term "progressive" as a euphemistic cover for their radical socialist ideas and policies.

The new liberalism is reactionary and retrogressive. It is retrogressive because it promotes a return to the principles of the ancient tyrannies of the past, to absolute governmental power in the hands of one person or one small class of people. It is also retrogressive because it enthrones and fosters the same evils that destroyed past civilizations: immorality, corruption, thievery, violence, greed, atheism, selfishness, and the rejection of Christianity and the traditional family. It ignores and discredits honest, objective historical research and strives to rewrite history to justify its own biases and to achieve the personal agendas of its proponents. This is called "revisionist history."

In America, the goals of the Left have been to propagandize the people with their destructive ideals and values, and to write their doctrines into law. In other words, their hallmark characteristic is to force their will upon all Americans by the power of the state.

As I noted above, conservatives desire to improve the world by improving the individual, but the Left desires to improve the world through government—and the individual be damned.

Progressives consider the Constitution to be outdated and irrelevant in the face of modern needs, so they constantly strive to deprive Americans of their constitutional rights. They endeavor to undermine the First Amendment, which guarantees all American citizens (not foreign nationals) the freedom to practice their religious beliefs without interference from the government or special interest groups. They also seek to destroy free speech in this country and characterize all speech they dislike as "hate speech."

They attack the Second Amendment, which guarantees individual citizens the right to keep and bear arms, and they do this by incessantly proposing useless and ineffective gun control measures, ratcheting up their rhetoric each time some maniac uses a gun to murder innocent people.

And by subtle and devious arguments, they have also erected an imaginary wall between church and state, thus preventing any type of religious expression in public schools.

In general, true conservatives are constitutionalists while liberals are anti-Constitution, although they hypocritically refer to that document when it furthers their agenda.

Most important, the actions of the leftist radicals have caused a tragic loss of goodness, freedom, and prosperity in America. If Americans do not stop these ideologues soon, they may lose forever the precious freedoms they hold so dear.

CHAPTER ONE

The Nature and Motivation of Leftists

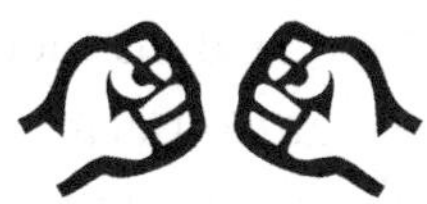

LIBERALS, PROGRESSIVES, AND LEFTISTS ARE basically the same.

In this book, the terms liberals, progressives, and leftists are used interchangeably. Yes, there are technical differences between them, but the ideologies of all these groups are similar and only differ in the degree to which they lean to the left. The closer they get to the ultimate leftist doctrine of Marxism, the more radical they become. If we put the Left on a spectrum, it begins with modern-day liberalism (as opposed to classical liberalism), then progressivism, and finally full-fledged radical leftism.

Liberals are profoundly brainwashed.

You may be surprised if I say that it is very unlikely you will ever be able to convince leftists of anything. But it is true. The reason for this is that they are so indoctrinated with Marxist ideology and leftist doctrines that they eventually become unable to think independently. They usually adopt and cherish the commonly received notions of political correctness. Often they are brainwashed almost to the point of total psychological stupor. They receive this indoctrination and brainwashing virtually everywhere in our society, from teachers in schools, the media, the entertainment industry, the medical establishment, social scientists, politicians, political pundits, and a plethora of so-called experts.

Whatever causes liberals to behave the way they do, the results can be truly devastating. Many of them act as if they were completely insane, screaming, ranting angrily, waving their arms violently, scolding, accusing, blowing whistles, tearing down signs, stomping their feet, breaking windows, physically attacking perceive enemies, and refusing to listen to any questions or engage in any reasonable discussion. At the same time, many "learned," high-profile liberals strive to present the image of being objective and rational, but in the final analysis they show themselves to be smug, condescending, self-righteous, elitist, and all-around bullies.

The problem is that liberal doctrines and policies have permeated our institutions and the psyche of the people to such a degree that nearly every citizen of the Western World has been corrupted to some degree. This insidious brainwashing has proceeded unabated for over a hundred and fifty years, and only a small number of patriots are fighting it. Thankfully, the ranks of these patriots are growing in number.

Leftists seldom have a serious knowledge of the issues but take for granted what they are told through the ubiquitous propaganda from the people and institutions I have listed above. The media especially has been successful in creating universal notions of what is acceptable and what is not, and these acceptable beliefs include medical correctness, science correctness, social correctness, religious correctness, and of course political correctness.

Are all conservatives immune to the negative propaganda that pervades society? Are they innocent of the faults displayed by leftists? Definitely not. They too have been influenced by the ideology of the Left to some degree or another, and frequently they unknowingly and blindly repeat or even support leftist doctrines. It has been a sad but instructive experience for me to debate with many of these potential patriots.

Even good, honorable people of all persuasions may inadvertently and ignorantly promote liberal ideology and thus advance the destruction of peace, prosperity, and liberty. Most of these decent people do not actively engage in the fight, and there are many reasons for this. Some do not realize the seriousness of the problem because they are so busy making a living and raising a family that they are too tired and harassed to inform themselves. Others spend most of their nonwork hours engaging in various types of enjoyable amusements. Still others are simply the gullible believers in whatever the media says.

Liberal motivation

What motivates liberals, and why is it that they seem so devoid of a sense of humor? These things are difficult to ascertain. Why do liberals tend so easily to become furious and even hateful when anyone disagrees with them? Why do many of them so quickly resort to insults, name-calling, hatred, anger, disruption, and violence? Several reasons have been suggested by psychologists and others who have studied the difficulty. Their answers vary from poor nurturing in their youth to an inherent love of evil.

Some researchers believe that liberals have deep-seated psychological problems, often stemming from their childhood. In other words, their psychopathology.[2]

At times leftists seem to be controlled by the spirit of evil and to seek to accomplish their designs in any way they can, including lies, violence, murder, and the manipulation of others. In other words, for them the ends justify the means.

It is difficult to accept the idea that pure evil can reside in the hearts of some, and no government program or cultural movement can stop their actions. Some killers are simply pathological monsters, but most societal mayhem has been caused by ideological fanatics. For leftists, their doctrines are a sacred religion.

---

2 Lyle Rossiter, *The Liberal Mind*, pp. 403-406.

Other researchers believe that these radicals are manipulated by powerful operators behind the scenes, conspirators who spend billions striving to destroy individual freedom and Western Civilization. The Left loves to call these researchers "conspiracy theorists" as if real conspiracies do not exist and as if that claim was a valid argument.

It may be true that all these factors play a role, to some degree or another, in the makeup of the modern-day liberal.

There is one crucial factor that is usually overlooked by writers who are challenging the tactics of the Left, and that is the use of drugs—prescribed drugs, over-the-counter drugs, and illegal drugs. History shows that many of the mass shootings are perpetrated by sick people who hold radical, leftist political views and whose brains are "fried" on drugs. Often they are hooked on antidepressants, prescribed for them legally.

All of these people are eventually examined by medical doctors and psychiatrists, who, of course, always decline to assign any blame to the very drugs they prescribe. In fact, they never even mention drugs in their reports on the mental state of mass murderers. These shooters display all the signs of mental psychosis, and religious and ideological fanatics typically exhibit the same type of behavior.

Most of all, leftists have great difficulty in discerning between truth and falsehood and between right and wrong. In connection with this, it may be worthwhile for us to analyze what truth is.

Truth describes something that exists in reality. Reality is the real world that is constant and eternal. Therefore, truth is absolute and immutable. It contrasts sharply with the ever-changing flux of men's opinions, emotions, and discoveries. An infinite number of truths exist which never conflict with one another, and all men should strive to grasp and embrace them. Everything in the world depends on truth, including human values, love, beauty, knowledge, progress, and happiness.

The pathway to truth can be extremely arduous, and negotiating it takes great dedication and effort. Why? Because one must strive to weed out all apparent truths, conflicting theories, and false "facts." People sometimes claim that truth varies with the individual, and that individual perceptions on a given subject may be equally true even if they seem to contradict one another. This is the dangerous, false doctrine of relative truth, a belief whose source is Satan. It states that each person can have his "truth," which is just as valid as the "truths" of others. As a result, the individual has no consistent guiding light other than personal feelings, and thus believers in relative truth fall into all kinds of error and destructive behavior.

Even though truth may be difficult to find, you will recognize it when you find it because it will come to you as if in a sudden revelation. That truth will be supremely simple, open up great vistas, explain new things, and bring you peace and joy.

Fortunately, God has given man many wonderful tools to ascertain truth, including intuition (that gut instinct), common sense, inspiration, intelligence, personal discernment, special talents and gifts, the power to use reason and logic, and the ability to engage in empirical, scientific research.

What factors can prevent man from grasping truth? If our heart is impure, our intent dishonest, our life corrupt and immoral, our reasoning altered by excessive passion, our decisions based on personal prejudices and foolish indoctrination, or if we lust for power and wealth, then it will be very difficult for us to recognize truth. Our job then must be to rid ourselves of these destructive impediments. To fail to do so will result in bringing misery to ourselves and help create a dysfunctional society.

This explains in part why many liberals cannot see, understand, and accept truth when directly confronted with it: they are blinded by the corruption of their personal lives.

Christ is the ultimate source and embodiment of all truth. As Jesus said, "I am the way, the truth, and the life." (John 14:6) He also declared, "Ye shall know the truth, and the truth shall make you free." (John 8:32) Free from what? From error, darkness, despair, corruption, and endless disappointment. So those who do not believe in a law-giving God have much difficulty ascertaining the truth.

The Job of Conservatives

Therefore, our job as conservatives is not to try to convince die-hard leftists of anything because they tend to be closed-minded and see themselves as already knowing everything. Our real job is to influence, and hopefully convert, people who are still relatively open-minded and those who are monitoring the debate. If we are lucky, sometimes we can persuade wishy-washy, trickle-down liberals who are still searching, if such a creature actually exists.

Only people who have been diligent in learning the meaning of true freedom and genuine American history and traditions are relatively free from liberal indoctrination. The purpose of this book is to support their efforts in the struggle to defeat the tactics and the lies of the Left.

Liberals Classified

In any case, it is important that we try to categorize liberals according to the degree of their dedication to leftist causes. In their excellent book, *Waking the Sleeping Giant*, published in 2012, Drs. Gary Casselman and Timothy Daughtry divide American voters into several categories as of 2012:

- Of mainstream voters, 40% do not identify as either conservative or liberal.
- Of mainstream voters, another 40% register as conservatives.
- The remaining 20% of voters claim to be liberals.

Casselman and Daughtry put the 20% of liberals into three categories:

- **Hard core liberals**

The authors estimate that 1% of the liberals are hard core. These people have completely embraced the doctrines of the left.

They have rejected the ideals of Judeo-Christianity and get their marching orders from Marxism, Nietzsche, and Darwin. They are so completely brainwashed that it is unlikely they will ever change, and if you get stuck debating with them, you can expect them to immediately reject everything you say. Many of them know that liberalism and socialism are destructive false philosophies, but they simply do not care because if they can win the ideological battle, they will be able to exalt themselves to great wealth, power, and popularity. In other words, they purposely conspire against America.

- Uninformed liberals

The remaining 19% of liberals are considered as either uninformed or misinformed liberals. The uninformed liberals care little about politics, but are victims of institutional and trickle-down liberalism. They usually vote for liberal candidates because they feel it is the popular thing to do. These people can sometimes be swayed by logic and evidence showing the inconsistencies of liberal doctrines.

- Misinformed liberals

The misinformed liberals are victims of informational and trickle-down liberalism. They have greater interest in social and political issues than the uninformed and consider themselves to be quite knowledgeable. They can be swayed in the same way as uninformed voters, but are harder to convince.[3]

Of course, the lines between the uninformed and misinformed can be blurred depending on the issues and the circumstances. To the categories just reviewed, I might add two others: conservative liberals and liberal conservatives. These are people who express support of both liberal and conservative policies at the same time. Conservative liberals support most liberal policies but are

---

3 Casselman and Daughtry, *Waking the Sleeping Giant*, pp. 15, 35, 39, 76-77, 116, 124.

conservative in their personal lives and will promote of few aspects of the conservative platform. Liberals conservatives embrace conservative values, but sometimes vote for liberal candidates.

In this book, I seek to refute the doctrines of hard core liberals and to destroy their self-confidence, to influence and perhaps persuade the uniformed and the misinformed voters and, at the same time, confirm conservatives in their convictions. It is possible that some of the same people who fight everything you say now will someday remember your words and change their belief system.

More so than conservatives, liberals tend to

- rely on excessive emotion.
- be deeply offended by any idea that challenges their biases.
- lack facts.
- consider their opinions and feelings to be facts.
- consider their factoids to be absolutely true.
- believe ferociously and adamantly that the few things they do know are the ultimate truth.
- be illogical.
- show arrogance and display their superior virtue.
- act childishly.
- display demagoguery.
- exhibit severe signs of brainwashing.
- be a bit crazy in the noggin.
- love to use dopey slogans and signs.
- frequently employ insults and name-calling.
- promote fake conspiracy theories.
- do dubious "fact-checking."
- be unemployed.
- live in their parents' basement.
- possess only a short list of talking points that they repeat endlessly.
- refuse to engage in rational arguments but use shouting and heckling instead.

- believe in moral relativism and their own truth.
- resort to direct confrontations and violence.
- typically show mastery of tricky language, lies, and misrepresentations.
- despise and belittle conservatives and even other liberals who are not as radical (dedicated) as they should be.
- believe the most outlandish and implausible nonsense.
- worship destructive and false doctrines like socialism and Marxism.
- become gaga over the most moronic statements of their nuttiest leaders.
- create or follow sitcoms, TV series like Star Trek, and movies in which they can finally be right, get justification for their personal behavior, really "win" arguments, and realize their imaginary fantasy world.[4]

Star Trek is of course an immensely entertaining and well-loved TV series for people across the entire political spectrum. The liberal indoctrination is very crafty and hardly felt even by confirmed conservatives. As a result, the viewers are led to have no problem with a future multiglobal government called the Federation of Planets that rules supreme without being approved by the vote of its citizens. In fact, the citizens do not elect anyone. Viewers witness star travelers sleeping together without the benefit of marriage, and doctors in Sick Bay magically cure people suffering from lethal diseases with a blinking flashlight and even resurrecting the dead.

As Ann Colter said, Star Trek and most other mediums of entertainment have been highjacked by liberals to subtly promote their agendas.

Even an innocuous TV series like "The Andy Griffith Show," in Season 2, Episode 24, presents a beautiful (of course) county

---

4 Ann Colter, *How to Talk to a Liberal (If You Must)*, pp. 4-6.

nurse, a brunette named Mary Simpson, who is dedicated to her campaign to vaccinate everyone in the county for tetanus by hook or crook. As a result, she succeeds and is lauded by everyone as a fine hero.

CHAPTER TWO

The Left's Causes

LIBERALS CONSISTENTLY FOR THE BAD and seldom for the good, and because of this, all they see is the bad. They seem to have no sense of proportion and little sense of humor when it comes to politics. That suggests they are deeply disillusioned with life and can never be satisfied with anything. This lack of satisfaction causes them to constantly engage in promoting foolish causes and making demands that are outlandish, ludicrous, irrelevant, and simply impossible.

Even if they realize their crazy goals are totally impossible, they pursue them anyway to satisfy their emotional need for relevance. But the great problem is that all their expectations and demands are destructive to freedom and American society. What follows is part of the liberal wish list.

The radical Left wants to convince the world that:

- God does not exist and that traditional religion, especially Christianity, is destructive.
- intelligent people should advocate for the spread and glorification of atheism.
- there is no absolute truth because everything is relative.

- since there is no absolute truth, individuals can have their own truth.
- only feelings and emotions are truly valid and have worth.
- we should glorify love and beauty above facts and truth.
- people should honor, accept, and promote homosexual rights.
- the feelings and "rights" of the LGBTQ community and the transgender crowd are legitimate, and therefore these people should get special privileges, even if it deprives others of their rights.
- gay marriage is good, moral, and legitimate.
- we must educate females (indoctrinate them) and promote tax-funded family planning (abortion and contraception).
- we must defend women's right to do with their bodies what they want and to have abortions on demand.
- abortion is good, moral, and legitimate.
- sexual freedom (immorality) should be enshrined.
- if you do not happily embrace and promote every form of sexual perversion, they will ridicule you and try to destroy your life.
- it is a fact (fantasy) that your gender is what you want it to be in spite of biological reality.
- sex is biological, but gender is a (made-up) social construct.
- the idea of male and female, two genders only, is cruel, discriminatory and sexist.
- it is true that women have always been subordinate to men and still are, that men are at fault, and that this discrimination needs to be exposed and stopped.
- women should receive equal pay in spite of the fact that they make different career choices from men.
- government welfare and the redistribution of wealth is just, honorable, kind, and equitable.
- worldwide socialism, and Communism are necessary and highly desirable.
- global governance and the elimination of national borders

are inevitable and desirable in spite of the fact that they would destroy individual freedom and facilitate the spread of worldwide pandemics like coronaviruses and even more lethal diseases.

- we must abolish capitalism and embrace socialism or Communism.
- cultural diversity and multiculturalism are good and must be promoted.
- tolerance of evil is good and intolerance of evil is bad.
- we should all be tolerant of others no matter what they do or what they support.
- it is proper to discredit the US Constitution and the Founding Fathers, calling them outdated and old-fashioned.
- history (revisionist history) proves America has always been racist, sexist, violent, warmongering, and not great at all.
- the idea that America is the greatest, freest, kindest, and most prosperous nation in history should be rejected. America has never been a great country.
- since America is not perfect, you are justified in hating and destroying it.
- more gun control is needed to save lives.
- guns should eventually be confiscated because they are a symbol of destructive and selfish individualism.
- everyone should despise the ideas of patriotism, nationalism, American exceptionalism, and national sovereignty in favor of a global world of peace, happiness, equality, and fairness (global tyranny).
- everyone should promote the use of GMOs.
- Americans must defend Common Core in schools (government indoctrination).
- America should prosecute and possibly imprison homeschoolers who defy the law. In other words, we must punish those who refuse to have their children indoctrinated by the collectivist public school system.

- everyone on the planet should promote the belief that man-made global warming is an imminent existential threat to mankind (read, an unmitigated scam).
- we must support the green new deal to save the world from extinction in twelve years.
- because of global warming, we only have a dozen years or so before mankind will end, unless we stop using fossil fuels, completely overhaul industry and commerce, and surrender the sovereignty of all nations to the UN.
- by means of government laws and regulations, we must stop the exploitation and degradation of the environment.
- we must advance the principle of open borders in order to welcome into the US and Europe the world's poor.
- whites are responsible for the slavery, persecution, and poverty of minorities.
- we must push the cause of Muslims and Islam or be called racist, even though the word Muslim refers to a religion not to an ethnic group.
- Americans and the world should promote pharmaceuticals and vaccines as the cure of all or most diseases even though they treat only symptoms.
- vaccines are safe and effective even if they destroy the natural immune system.
- all people everywhere should join together to defeat right-wing extremism.
- race warfare still exists in America.
- America has always been a racist, sexist, Islamophobic, and xenophobic nation.
- profiling is racist because the police target people of color.
- reparations should be paid to Indians and blacks.
- America must make large, greedy corporations accountable.
- we should force the rich to pay their fair share.
- we ought to place industries like finance and health care under democratic control (control of the elite).

- we all should struggle for social justice.
- the people should promote the concept that the working class is exploited by big business.
- we must support unions, no matter how activist they are.
- we have to eliminate the Electoral College.
- we need to advance the just doctrine of equality of outcome (through welfare).
- we need to downplay the doctrine of equality of opportunity (individual initiative).
- we must use the (brute) force of government to abolish all poverty, inequality, unhappiness, oppression, war, xenophobia, sexism, and racism.
- we need to provide job security and economic security for all and a living wage for the poor.
- we should give free health care to all, even illegal immigrants.
- we should furnish free education for all.
- we must cancel all student loan debts.
- we must provide physical and mental security for all.
- we must support decent, affordable housing for all.
- we should meet the special needs of seniors no matter how wealthy they are.
- we must promote a fulfilling life for everyone.
- we should create a fair, just, and more humane society.
- we must put people before profits.
- America should downplay national defense and the military.
- we must reject putting America first because that destroys our duty to the world.
- we must look to big government as the solution to all problems (that is, promote socialism and Communism).

Well now, that is an extremely aggressive and all-inclusive agenda, isn't it? Talk about yearning for an imaginary Utopia! All of these multifaceted desires are complex and interrelated, but still they are certainly fair, reasonable, and completely possible in the liberal mind. All we need to do is tax the Haves to the tune of a hundred trillion dollars, or have the Treasury quickly print the money needed, and do all these marvelous things through a kind, responsible, efficient, and benign central government, especially one controlled by the Democrats and other liberals. No problem at all!

It is just as easy as having Star Trek's godlike Q snap his fingers to perform impossible miracles, isn't it?

If all or a significant portion of this agenda were accomplished, that would be the end of freedom and civilized society throughout the world. Poverty, degradation, injustice, tyranny, and slavery would reign supreme.

CHAPTER THREE

Primary Tactics of the Left: Tricky Language

The Left spends a great deal of time, money, and effort developing ways of promoting their disastrous causes and defeating, demonizing, or "canceling" any person or group that opposes them. Their disruptive tactics seem almost endless, and the list is growing every day.

Here are their two primary tactics (with synonyms):

- evasion (diversion, deviation, deflection, dodging, and circumvention)
- bullying (browbeating, canceling, threatening, discrediting, disrupting, intimidating, assaulting, and murdering)

By means of evasion, leftists are freed from the necessity of providing cogent arguments. They can avoid responding to questions, skirt around the issues, make irrelevant comments, throw up distracting, confusing smoke screens, and save face.

In this book I present lists of their favorite evasion tactics, which I divide into two general categories:

- evasion through tricky language manipulation, presented in this chapter and called "slogans."

- evasion through deceptive content independent of popular slogans, presented in Chapter Four and called "strategies."

By bullying, the Left can force its will on everyone else. The primary instruments of this bullying are organized groups like Antifa, brainwashed students, the power of big government, and conspiring globalists. Examples of bullying are included in our lists of evasion. I have not separated examples of bullying from examples of evasion because both tactics are often entertwined in liberal attacks.

As previously mentioned, progressives are masters at creating Teflon definitions. In other words, if a term loses its impact in furthering their agenda, they simply alter the meaning of that term or adopt another, more effective word. Then they instruct their lapdogs in the media and other institutions to repeat the new terms ad infinitum until a blind, gullible public finally accepts them as politically correct and the absolute truth. What follows is a list of a few of the hundreds of deceptive linguistic slogans liberals use.

Slogan 1: "Liberalism will save mankind."

At first the Left adored the term liberal because it sounded so wonderful. After all, "liberal" implied openness, generosity, and freedom. It was even inaccurately conflated with the classical liberalism of the Founding Fathers. But then, over the decades of the 20th century, the word gradually took on negative connotations because conservatives, libertarians, and moderates began to convince the public that liberalism was associated with big government, welfare, and many other anti-American values.

So, the Left conveniently abandoned the word liberal and started calling themselves "progressives." That term was even more impressive because it suggested change, growth, hope, and newness. Unfortunately, the Left, with their brand-new name proceeded, just as before, to undermine American values, traditions, and history.

Slogan 2: "Global Warming will soon kill us all. Don't you believe in climate change?"

By the term "global warming" progressives are referring to their unsubstantiated claim that the increase in average planetary temperatures is largely caused by man's use of fossil fuels and the consequent creation of dangerous levels of carbon dioxide, and this increase will soon destroy all life on earth. In twelve years at this writing.[5]

It is true that global warming does occur. The earth's average temperature has been rising and falling for millions of years. It always rises after every ice age. The Little Ice Age ended around 1850, and temperatures have climbed since then, but only a degree or two. In addition, there is no proof that the small rise is caused by human activities or that mankind is in danger.

However, when temperatures began to level out around 1999, and the temperature increase was minimal for the next twenty-two years, the progressives faced a dilemma. So they simply changed their vocabulary; instead of man-made global warming they used "man-made climate change." Why? Because they realized that it was easy to prove the climate was changing for the simple reason that over vast time periods, the climate has always been changing.

The new designation of "climate change" also allowed warmists to claim that people who teach the climate is not changing in dangerous ways will automatically be wrong, and the Left can legitimately call those people "climate deniers"—as evil as the deniers of the Holocaust—while they continue to push for huge carbon taxes on the Western World.

In spite of this, the warmers have not been getting the traction they hoped for in public opinion, and they realized they needed to

5 John Stossel, "Are We Doomed?" Nov. 19, 2019, 5:57, https://www.youtube.com/watch?v=b8JZo6PzpCU.

make the warming much more frightening, so they invented new attention-getting terms like "climate crises" and "climate collapse" and "climate catastrophe."

The promotion of man-made global warming is nothing more than a deceitful effort of leftist governments and globalists to grab power and control over the world's economies.

Slogan 3: "We must heal the climate and support climate justice."

This is another emotional appeal to impose huge carbon taxes on every taxpayer on the planet, especially American taxpayers.

Slogan 4: "We need to be climate positive."

The global warming alarmists now use this buzz phrase to indicate that everyone should acknowledge that the globe is warming dangerously fast, and if they do, they'll be working in the right direction. Bill Nye, the "Science Guy," is a typical example of the global warming fanatics. He claims that global warming is undeniable, that the science is settled, and so foolish skeptics should stop debating and questioning it. They should just accept the overwhelming scientific evidence that human activity is causing accelerated climate changes on a time scale of years.[6, 7]

If they do not do so, they are science deniers and are suffering from cognitive dissonance. In the past, Nye has said that climate deniers should be imprisoned as war criminals.

The position of global warming alarmists is based on nothing but fake, junk science.

Slogan 5: "America is a democracy."

Democracy is the Left's deceitful term for "mob rule." America

---

6 Tucker Carlson, "Tucker vs. Bill Nye the Science Guy," *Fox News*, Feb. 27, 2017, 9:22, https://www.youtube.com/watch?v=qN5L2q6hfWo.

7 Piers Morgan, "Marc Morano on Global Warming," *CNN*, Dec. 4, 2012, 3:29, https://www.youtube.com/watch?v=yBg7PF-PBRM.

was originally founded as a republic, not a democracy. A more complete description would be that America was created as a constitutional representative federalist republic. But for over a hundred years the Left has spewed forth the propaganda that our nation is a democracy, and they want to make the world "safe for democracy."

However, a true democracy is one of the most freedom-destroying forms of government there is. It is essentially mob rule, where whatever the majority want and vote for at the moment they get, no matter how arbitrary or capricious it might be. That is one of the reasons why the Founding Fathers insisted on including the Bill of Rights in the Constitution—to protect the God-given rights of the minority.

In Federalist No. 10, James Madison, father of the Constitution, declared under the heading "Democracy" that "measures are too often decided, not according to the rules of justice and the rights of the minority party, but by the superior force of an interested and overbearing majority." It is easy for our "rulers" to manipulate the masses by the many effective means available today, and thus they are the ones who would hold ultimate power in a pure democracy.

Slogan 6: "Is our democracy up to the task of controlling climate change?"

In saying this, a senator from Colorado, Michael Bennet, a Democrat would-be contender for president, claimed that the main obstacle to his climate change agenda is democracy. Tucker Carlson, conservative news analyst, replied that democracy *is* the issue and that the senator is mad because that "damn democracy" is getting in the way of the desire of climate alarmists to control every detail of the lives of Americans.

But the leftists have a backup plan, Carlson explained, to bypass Congress: protests, youth climate strike groups, and comprehensive climate change "education" for children ages five through fourteen.[8, 9]

Climate researcher, Marc Morano, reports that in 2014 UN climate chief Christiana Figueres claimed that US democracy was "very detrimental" in the global warming battle and praised China for "doing it right" on climate change. Figueres added that "China is also able to implement policies because its political system avoids some of the legislative hurdles seen in countries including the U. S." In other words, Figueres believes an absolute oligarchy that denies the right of its people to vote and rules over them in tyranny is more effective than a democracy.[10]

Slogan 7: "They are undocumented, not illegal."

The term undocumented is LeftSpeak for illegal aliens, who are basically criminals. The Left enjoys lying by means of word choice, calling illegal aliens "undocumented workers." So now the responsibility no longer lies with the criminals, but with American society in general that neglects to document them. It is so much kinder that way. At any rate, people who sneak into our country without proper immigration documents are doing so illegally and thus are illegals.

Gary Johnson, 2016 Libertarian presidential candidate, was an example of this LeftSpeak when he told a reporter it was important that people use "undocumented immigrants" and not "illegal immigrants" because the word illegal was rude and might offend illegal Hispanics now living in the US.[11]

---

8 MSNBC, "2020 Dem Candidate Michael Bennet Complains 'Democracy' Is Getting In The Way Of Green New Deal," Sept. 19, 2019, 1:05, https://www.youtube.com/watch?v=Yser_K1-bwA.

9 Brittany Hughes, "No One With a Brain Takes Climate Alarmists Seriously - and Here's Why," *RealityCheck*, Sept. 23, 2019, https://www.youtube.com/watch?v=6jz60NUhiys.

10 Marc Morano, *Climate Change*, p. 230.

11 CBN News, "Brodie File Exclusive: Gary Johnson Won't Use Term 'Illegal Immigrants,' Says It's Hurtful Not Helpful," Sept. 13, 2016, 4:18, https://www.youtube.com/watch?v=U28inDioeOo.

Slogan 8: "We are pro-choice. You are anti-choice."

The first sentence is the Left's deceptive term for pro-abortion. The second is their term for people who oppose abortion. The Left enjoys lying by using euphemisms. Now women who murder their unborn babies are pro-choice not pro-abortion. That focuses on their supposed "rights and freedoms" and ignores the greater and more merciful right of the baby to life. You see, anything "anti-" has got to be much worse than anything "pro-."

Slogan 9: "You are against a woman's right to choose. Nobody has a right to tell me what to do with my body."

This is the radical feminists' excuse for murdering unborn babies. They worry only about their own bodies but avoid talking about the human bodies in their wombs. If they do not want a baby, then they should avoid getting pregnant.

Slogan 10: "They are fetuses, not babies."

Liberals who support abortion always call unborn babies "fetuses." In other words, just a clump of tissue cells. It is obvious that they do this to dehumanize the unborn so that when the unwanted child is torn apart in the womb, the doctors who perform the abortions and the women who submit to them will not feel so guilty. So with the sleight of linguistic hand, they justify the most murderous, barbaric practice on earth.

Slogan 11: "The unarmed Trayvon Martin, Michael Brown, or Eric Garner."

In nearly every news report by the liberal media about the killing of a black man named Michael Brown by police officer Darren Wilson, the commentators made sure to say the "Unarmed Michael Brown." It is truly uncanny how all of the reports used the exact same word—unarmed. In other words, the reporters seemed possessed to present only the evidence favoring Michael Brown.

The same was true of Trayvon Martin, after he was shot by George Zimmerman, who was an Hispanic defending his life.

Never did you hear this: "The threatening, belligerent Michael Brown" or "The aggressive Trayvon Martin." The impression is strong that a liberal bias was at work, coming from one central source. The same is true in the Eric Garner case. Here the reports stressed two things: Eric Garner was "strangled" and he was "unarmed." For example, one link to the Arkansas Times says: "No charge against New York officer who strangled unarmed man."[12]

So those news sources irrationally defended the "unfortunate" black men, who in fact were not innocent of wrongdoing, while condemning those who reportedly caused their deaths. They are still doing the same thing today.

Slogan 12: "You're racist because you called them colored people."

In LeftSpeak the use of the term "colored people" is obviously a sign of disgusting racism. Instead, you must use "people of color." If you do that, you are truly "woke" and thus a good little liberal.

Slogan 13: "I'm not voting because I don't like any of the candidates."

This sentiment is one of the saddest and most destructive positions a person can have. Destructive to oneself and to individual liberty. For thousands of years, nations, peoples, and tribes were governed by autocratic dictators, who made laws according to their personal whims. The common people were slaves or subjects who had no say in how they were governed. With the exception of some small scattered communities, universal suffrage did not exist during this dark and benighted era—for many millennia.

The natural tendency of any government is to grow and expand its power and influence. Even governments that started as relatively free republics eventually degenerated into totalitarian

---

12 Arkansas Blog, Arkansas news, politics, opinion . . . *Arkansas Times*, Nov. 3, 2014.

powers. Early examples of this are the ancient Greek democracy and the Roman Republic.

During the 18th century Age of Enlightenment, the light of freedom sprang forth once again, first in England and then in America with the Founding Fathers and the US Constitution. At that time most of the people could vote, and this right was gradually extended to the entire populace. This right was considered a cherished and long-hoped-for dream come true.

But today, many people are perfectly willing to forsake and abandon that sacred right and duty simply because they cannot identity their perfect candidate, as if any candidate were capable of being perfect for everyone. They sometimes say that they are "making a statement," a claim that is pure nonsense. I believe that people who choose not to vote are committing a form of suicide because they show little respect for their own freedom, their personal safety, and their right to property simply because, in their excessive idealism, they cannot have their way.

Slogan 14: "That legislation is divisive."

Whenever the liberal Left hates a piece of legislation, they typically call it divisive. A recent example is the Indiana SB 101, signed into law in March 2015, supporting religious freedom. To the Left, that law is divisive because it thwarts one of their pet agendas—gay rights. And anything that interferes with the supposedly sacred "rights" of gays makes most gays, and their brainwashed supporters, raise a nationwide ruckus. I oppose any type of violence against gays and I believe they should be free to live their lives as they see fit, but I object when the rainbow crowd begin to propagandize the world that their behavior is perfectly normal, that we are evil if we do not accept it as such, and when they push for legislation giving themselves special privileges.

Slogan 15: "We must put partisan politics aside."

So says Democrat Ben McAdams, representative from Utah's 4th congressional district.[13] Some Republicans say the same thing, but the slogan is essentially meaningless when it is used to cover up or justify partisan politics and especially liberal policies.

Slogan 16: "You are discriminating."

The supporters of gay rights and women's rights use the term "discrimination" whenever they perceive anyone trying to supposedly undermine those so-called rights. The question I ask is on what basis does the Left think that gay rights or women's rights trump the constitutional right of religious freedom? If a Christian baker, one who hates homosexuality on religious grounds, does not want to bake a cake topped by two gays, what gives government or anyone else the right to force him to do so? The gays focus only on their alleged rights but deny the baker his real First Amendment right to religious freedom and his right to run his bakery as he sees fit.

These gays and their supporters have a purposeful agenda: they want to force every American to do their bidding and to embrace homosexuality as a valid, healthy lifestyle. Proof of this is seen, in the present case, from the fact that those gays who want to get "married" can simply go down the street and find another baker who will bake their cake. The first baker is not preventing them from doing this.

And do not compare this to discrimination against blacks. The color of one's skin is not a matter of evil, but millions sincerely believe that homosexuality and gay marriage are evils.

Slogan 17: "If we are to have equal rights, then the poor should have a right to health, adequate housing, food, safe water, and the right to free education."

Liberals have invented dozens of "rights" that are not in the

---

13 Ben McAdams, "McAdams says it's time to put partisan politics aside," *Fox News*, May 26, 2019, 10:58, https://www.youtube.com/watch?v=E0bn2UzuRyw.

Constitution, and that other people have to pay for. The Founding Fathers believed that all should have equal rights under the law, not equal rights in an absolute sense. John Lofgren, author of *Atlas Shouts*, explained:

> They [the Left] believe rights involve the transfer of money and services and preferential treatment to certain groups who are "underrighted." The word "rights" has been perverted, by them, into something it was never intended to be, nor can it be, if you examine what equal rights means: if one person's skin color means they get an extra "right," then rights are not equal; they have become a privilege at that point. And two rights make a wrong . . . [14]

Slogan 18: "You whites have white privilege and white supremacy and that gives you unfair advantages."

This is an imaginary claim, especially since the 1960s. Even before the 1960s most whites had to struggle to get ahead. During the Great Depression, vast numbers of whites and other races had to stand in breadlines. As a child, in order to get a few pennies, I had to collect tinfoil gum wrappers and save used cooking grease to sell at local service stations. Our aunt and uncle moved in with us because my uncle could not earn a living, although he was a skilled carpenter. We lived hand to mouth.

When I was a young teenager, I found it necessary to insert newspaper into my shoes when the soles wore out because we could afford only one new pair of shoes each year. As I grew up, I obtained one menial job after another, and later I did odd jobs to work myself through college. Eventually, however, my wife and I created our own small business to support ourselves. We refused all government and church assistance.

---

14 John Lofgren, *Atlas Shouts*, p. 129.

My wife had it even worse than I. Her family owned no home of their own but lived with relatives, and they were constantly moving from state to state in search of work. She and her sisters got only one present for Christmas and one for birthdays. Most of the time they went barefoot to save wear and tear on their shoes, which they eventually had to repair with tape.

I believe that what I describe above has been the lot of most lower and middle class white families, and the same is true even now. Only the wealthy seemed to have it better.

So, where is all the white privilege I hear liberals talk about?

Liberals harp constantly on this theme in order to con us into accepting government power to redistribute wealth from the Haves to the Have Nots. The following references discuss the claim of white supremacy.[15]

Candace Owens, a conservative black woman, said, "The definition of white supremacy has shifted. It just means that anybody that disagrees with the Left, anybody that dares venture away from Democrat ideology" [is a white supremacist].[16]

Slogan 19: "Check your privilege."

This is another "clever" expression liberals use to blame whites for having some mystical white privilege. It is true that in early American history whites possessed many privileges denied to minorities or whites of targeted ethnicities such as the Irish, but those privileges have disappeared for the most part. Today, one often gets the impression that blacks and Hispanics receive more special favors than whites, as we saw in the leftist program of affirmative action. But liberals have not abandoned the idea of white privilege. The conclusion is that if you have white privilege, then everyone else is

15 Lauren Southern: "Literally Everything is White Supremacy," *Rebel News*, Sept. 22, 2016, 4:40, https://www.youtube.com/watch?v=TiuWKiq2d8o.

16 Candace Owens, "BEAST MODE: Candace Owens SHUTS DOWN Her Protesters," *Huckabee*, Sept. 4, 2018, 5:45, https://www.youtube.com/watch?v=OzTt-xBY5tY&t=29s.

a victim, and it is your fault, so shut up. All this nonsense is used to silence the opposition and to compensate for weak arguments.[17]

Slogan 20: "It's femicide, not homicide."

Feminists and other leftists are not only the thought police, but also the word police. When a woman is killed, all of us must now call it "femicide " because "homicide" refers only to the killing of a man. The truth is, however, the term homicide comes from the Latin word homo, which means "human being," which—when I last checked—includes women.

Slogan 21: "Hah, Sir, I love your mansplaining."

Feminists have invented a new term called "mansplaining." When men disagree with them or other leftists, they frequently accuse those men of mansplaining, which they see as arrogant, patronizing, and condescending. And men who do that should shut up because they are not only privileged, rude bigots, but obviously wrong.[18, 19]

The truth is, however, that women who use that tactic are sexist, hypocritical, and engaging in self-pity because they know they have no valid arguments and must discredit their male opponents at all costs. Many examples of this tactic are found on YouTube.

Slogan 22: "Gender is a social construct."

"Social construct" is a fancy, made-up term to justify a lie. There

---

17 Lauren Southern, "Check your [white] privilege. 'White privilege' is a dangerous myth," *Rebel Media*, May 19, 2015, 5:32, https://www.youtube.com/watch?v=rvEvJaF0w2o.

18 FairFax Media, "Woman accusing a man of 'mansplaining' gets as good as she gives," Feb. 10, 2016, 2:27, https://www.youtube.com/watch?v=TJyQpRfaGnw.

19 Tucker Carlson, "WOW . . . Feminist accuses Tucker of 'mansplaining' on Kavanaugh - Tucker Carlson," *Fox News*, 10/16/18, 7:47, https://www.youtube.com/watch?v=t6pNxshjQMQ.

are not multiple genders, but only two. Those two correspond to what biology teaches us: there are only two sexes, male and female. This doctrine of multiple genders has been promoted by radical feminists and confuses children, seriously damages their self-worth, and inhibits their ability to grow up as healthy, responsible adults.

Slogan 23: "Migrants are pilgrims."

The leftist media calls the hundreds of thousands of Syrian migrants swarming into Europe "pilgrims," as if they were devout believers seeking Allah in Mecca. The word pilgrim lends nobility and honor to their "cause." Other more realistic observers simply call them migrants or even "invaders." The latter term is probably more accurate because most of the migrants are younger men without families. True pilgrims do not leave their families behind.

Why haven't these invaders fought for the freedom they claim to seek in their homelands? Many believe it is a calculated crusade of radical Islam to inject their influence and their Shariah law directly into Christian nations. They know they cannot conquer democratic nations, so they simply infiltrate them and provide justification for that invasion by pleading with the world to recognize their so-called plight and their terrible suffering.

We get the same nonsense from people who say that we should increase the burden on our welfare system by welcoming open immigration of Hispanics and give amnesty to those who are already here illegally.

Slogan 24: "Those refugees are asylum seekers."

Asylum refers to protection from arrest and extradition and is given especially to political refugees by a nation or by an embassy or other agency enjoying diplomatic immunity. However, today, most of those seeking asylum are not genuine refugees fleeing from persecution and danger, but are illegals seeking American welfare and American jobs. Nonetheless, the left-wing refugee lobby went into high gear at the end of 2019, playing on the public's natural compassion for suffering people to promote the acceptance of more illegals into this country.[20]

Slogan 25: "Anecdotes are not data."

One of the newest aberrations of the Left is to claim that anecdotes are not data. Here again, liberals make up their own rules and demand that everyone follow them. However, anyone with a smidgeon of intelligence can quickly see through this falsehood. And yet, this distortion is deceptively tricky because of the liberals' creative use of the terms anecdote and data.

Progressives talk as though an anecdote is something like a fairy tale without any real basis in reality. At the same time, they treat data as if it were absolute truth. But neither of these contentions is true.

Webster's dictionary defines anecdote as "a usually short narrative of an interesting, amusing, or biographical incident." Doesn't that sound like a verifiable story and not a fairy tale? That story may actually turn out to be a fact, especially if many people attest to it.

Webster's defines data as "factual information used as a basis for reasoning, discussion, or calculation." Thus data is not absolute truth, but factual information that may lead to truth.

So, when does an anecdote become data? That occurs when there are multiple anecdotes that say the same thing. If there are a large number of personal stories contending that vaccines contribute to autism, that becomes valid data. If many mass murders are committed by crazies on psychotropic drugs, that becomes valid data. On the issue of vaccines, there are thousands of similar anecdotes. On the issue of mass murders, there are hundreds, if not

---

20 William F. Jasper, "The Last Word: don't buy the 'refugee' compassion con," *The New American*, Jan. 20, 2020, p. 44.

thousands, of similar anecdotes. All of these anecdotes combined are, in fact, data.

Slogan 26: "I didn't lie, I misremembered or misspoke."

These are humorous terms lefties use to justify outright lying. NBC anchor Brian Williams was simply misremembering when he lied for twelve years about his being in a helicopter hit by enemy fire in Iraq as well as many other disingenuous lies.[21] Also, in 2016 presidential candidate Hillary Clinton claimed she came under sniper fire in Bosnia, but later adjusted her claim by saying she was "sleep deprived" and "misspoke" when making that comment.[22] However, she told the same story over and over. The truth is, these people were simply lying.

Slogan 27: "Conservatives are obstructionists."

The Left calls anyone who has honest problems with their ideas and policies "obstructionist." According to Bernie Sanders, a typical socialist, Republicans fought to obstruct all the good things Barack Obama was trying to do.[23]

Slogan 28: "Donald Trump is divisive."

Anyone who disagrees with the Left's ideas and policies is called "divisive." Trump is constantly divisive because he upsets many parts of the leftist agenda. In the following video The Washington Post presents a load of false statistics concerning Trump's first year in office.[24]

---

21 Sean Hannity, "Brian Williams Misremembers," *Fox News*, Media Research Center, Feb. 10, 2015, 8:30, https://www.youtube.com/watch?v=AZJfxH6upxs.

22 Sharyl Attkinsson, "Clinton's Bosnia Blunder," *CBS*, March 25, 2008, 2:56, https://www.youtube.com/watch?v=SfaxA9Q-9AQ.

23 Bernie Sanders, "Obstructionists," *MSNBC, The ED Show*, Dec. 9, 2011, 5:11, https://www.youtube.com/watch?v=bTUMHxthpRY.

24 *Washington Post,* "Trump's divisive first year in office," Jan. 19, 2018, 4:34, https://www.youtube.com/watch?v=M6zc1JZzdMU.

Slogan 29: "You are using hate speech."

Hate speech is the Left's term for any speech they do not like. It is an effort to silence conservatives and deprive them of their First Amendment right of free speech.[25]

Slogan 30: "Profiling is evil."

Progressives use this statement to undermine the police in their efforts to control crime, especially when a person of color is involved. Basically, they are accusing the police of targeting blacks and thus being racist and unjust. But the truth is, profiling may be good police work. The police have learned that—in certain places, times, and circumstances—certain ethnic groups are the people who will most likely commit crimes. It is only good police work for them to be more suspicious of those groups.

In Terry v. Ohio (1968) the Supreme Court ruled that a police officer has the authority to stop and frisk any person if the officer has reasonable suspicion that the person might commit a crime. The act of stopping and frisking is just a brief pat down to search for weapons. There is evidence that this practice has prevented many crimes.

Slogan 31: "That leader is polarizing the nation."

To polarize is to break people up into opposing factions or groups. When the media and liberal politicians dislike a political candidate, or anyone they oppose, they typically claim that he or she is "polarizing." Those who use this accusation do not bother to investigate the facts of the matter, but immediately jump to this conclusion in an unfair political tactic.

Slogan 32: "Those polls are not certified."

The Democratic Party and other liberals love polls and sponsor

---

25 *Wall Street Journal*, "Post Election, Hate Speech Washes Across U.S.", Nov. 15, 2016, 2:54, https://www.youtube.com/watch?v=kXCu6CsgOts.

large numbers of them. Why? As a political tool to manipulate their base and other voting groups. Usually their polls are conducted by leftist news organizations like Time Magazine, USA Today, the New York Times, and CNN. These polls are typically biased, poorly done, and totally inaccurate. In 2016 the polls cited by the Democratic Party showed that there was a 98% chance that Hillary Clinton would win the election over Donald Trump. Of course, that did not happen.

Now the Democrats claim that the polls they sponsor on their own candidates for president should be "certified," but that idea is based on convoluted rules established by the Democratic National Committee and ignores other valid criteria regarding a candidate's chances of being chosen in the primaries, such as the number of donors supporting that candidate. This is a tactic used to eliminate primary candidates the party does not like.

Slogan 33: "Correlation is not causation."

This idea is used by the medical establishment to exonerate the MMR vaccine and other vaccines. The exoneration goes something like this: just because a child was given the MMR vaccine and shortly after shows definite signs of autism, that does not prove that the vaccine caused the onset of the disease. Why? Because correlation (association) is not causation. But this explanation is problematic.

It is true that the prior administration of MMR is not 100% proof that the vaccine caused or contributed to the disease, but if the child had no health problems before the inoculation, and the time interval was short, that suggests a high probability that the vaccine was at fault. The frequency with which the medical people use this sacred mantra is very strange because it only applies to vaccines. If a doctor prescribes any other drug, and the patient has adverse reactions, then the doctor will reduce the dosage, discontinue the drug, or prescribe another drug.

You might wonder what all this has to do with arguing with

leftists. This irrational defense of vaccines is used more and more by liberal government health agencies at all levels of jurisdiction to pass rules and laws mandating that people, especially school-age children, receive dozens of doses of many different vaccines. If the children do not receive the vaccinations, they are excluded from school until they do.

When government mandates things, people lose freedom. The claim is that these mandates are "for the greater good," a doctrine always used by tyrannical regimes.

Slogan 34: "Well, the flu vaccine just lacks optimal effectiveness."

This is leftist MedSpeak for "the flu vaccine is essentially worthless." Of course, nothing is ever said about the dangerous ingredients in the flu vaccine, including the deadly neurotoxins mercury, aluminum, and formaldehyde. When challenged on this point, the medical authorities declare that the levels of such adjuvants are far too low to be a danger. They forget to mention that those adjuvants tend to accumulate in the body as the individual gets regular yearly shots.

Slogan 35: "It's genetic."

This is what some doctors will tell you when they have no clue what you have or what your child has. In this way doctors do not have to "explain" what they do not understand. And guess what? Since your condition is caused by genetics (also called "family history," "inherited traits," etc.), then of course there are no natural medicines or healthy nutrition that can prevent, treat, or cure your condition. So all you can do is to trust your doctor to give you drugs (chemicals) to ease the terrible symptoms. Doctors seldom tell you that heredity does not cause any disease (with rare exceptions) but can only increase your susceptibility to certain diseases. If heredity is such an important factor, why then did our ancestors not have the same chronic diseases (heart trouble, diabetes, arthritis, etc,) to the same extent?

Slogan 36: "It's a medication."

These days doctors and drug companies frequently call natural supplements, such as vitamins, minerals, fish oil, probiotics, etc. "medications." Is this foolishness an effort to gain control of the distribution of supplements, charge more for them, and give people the impression they shouldn't take supplements without a doctor's permission?

Slogan 37: "Take charge of your life."

This comes from TV ads selling drugs. The reasoning goes something like this. If you have a health problem and you have no idea what is causing it, go to your doctor. He'll prescribe a drug he often knows almost nothing about but was convinced by a drug rep that it was effective for your problem.

Of course, the drug rep himself knows nothing about the human body or disease; he has just memorized cold everything his drug company employer taught him about two or three drugs. He can really spout off the "facts" regarding those two or three drugs, but that's all he knows.

Or the doctor will consult the Physicians Desk Reference which contains tens of thousands of drugs to choose a drug designed especially for you. A drug formulated to control symptoms, not to cure the disease. Of course, it is virtually impossible to find information on how many drugs are actually listed in the various editions of this book

So with your new, profound knowledge on how to solve your problem, you buy and take the drug. You trust the authority of the doctor so much that you do not even bother to read the voluminous insert provided by the pharmacist to learn what it will do, or what might be the side effects, and your doctor did not seem to feel it necessary to mention side effects at all.

So this is how you can "take charge of your life."

Slogan 38: "We should always promote human rights."

Conservatives should beware of the liberal appeal to an ever-growing laundry list of human rights, rights that are not found in the Constitution. Some of these rights include the right to Social Security, the right to free health care, the right to a free college education, a woman's right to have an abortion, and the right to paid vacations. However, the fundamental point here is that new territories are constantly being claimed as human rights as the Left comes up with new ideas about what they think might be nice for all human beings to have.

Slogan 39: "We are speaking truth to power."

Wikipedia says: "Speaking truth to power is a nonviolent political tactic, employed by dissidents against the received wisdom or propaganda of governments they regard as oppressive, authoritarian or an ideocracy."

But it is not usually "dissidents" who use this tactic, but liberals.

Today, liberals use this vainglorious expression to manipulate their base, to justify their policies, and especially to legitimize their opposition to President Donald Trump and to anyone they disagree with.[26]

Slogan 40: "Join the fight for good."

Evil always paints itself as good, and leftists are masters at it. Is promoting abortion, the murdering of millions of innocent unborn babies, good? Is inviting millions of illegal migrants into America good? Is endlessly attacking everything conservatives and the president do or say good? In doing these things, the liberals who use this catchphrase carefully avoid mentioning any of the disastrous policies promoted by past liberal politicians.

---

26 AM JOY, "AM Joy features Pam Keith speaking truth to power on gun violence," *MSNBC*, March 5, 2018, 5:58, https://www.youtube.com/watch?v=vYn95joZ4M8.

Slogan 41: "We ask everyone to be more thoughtful."

When Democrats and other liberals ask people to be more thoughtful, they really mean

they want people to remain silent or be more politically correct by supporting leftist causes.

Slogan 42: "We only want a more just and humane society."

This is another noble and pompous expression to describe the supposed, illusory benefits of progressivism, socialism and Communism.

Slogan 43: "You are racist."

Progressives call racist just about every person or policy or action that opposes their agenda. This is their favorite go-to tactic, and the convoluted logic they employ to arrive at that conclusion can be astounding. They see everything President Trump says, tweets, or does as racist without a shred of proof. If conservatives judge someone by their actions and character and not the color of their skin, liberals typically describe them as racist.

On social media I once criticized Sadiq Khan, the Muslim mayor of London, and a liberal expert countered, accusing me of being racist. I had to remind him that "Muslim" refers to a religious affiliation, not to a race.

The following reference highlights how the Left maintains power by manipulating blacks and the poor with lies about American racism and white supremacy.[27]

Slogan 44: "Trump is racist because he wants to ban Muslim migrants."

The Left constantly trumpets the idea of Trump being racist. But since Muslims are not a race but members of a religion called Islam, curtailing their immigration to the US cannot be racism.

As for President Trump's ban, he promoted a temporary ban

---

27 John Stossel, "The Lie of the Left," *LibertyPen,* Aug. 18, 2015, 4:44, https://www.youtube.com/watch?v=O_CH3w5SxDc.

on people from seven Middle East terrorist nations from flooding into the US like they are doing in Europe. The ban would be lifted when we were capable of properly vetting those immigrants. But liberals conveniently expand this idea and claim that Trump wants to ban all Muslims.[28]

However, if cutting immigration quotas from those countries should prove ineffective, it would be wise to ban all those who believe in the Muslim law of Sharia because it curtails the right of anyone to practice the religion of their choice, unless it is Islam.

Newt Gingrich, Republican politician, has suggested we deport all Muslims who believe in Shariah.[29] I would go further and say we should make them denounce Shariah publicly.

Slogan 45: "Islam is a religion of peace."

In order to be politically correct or to prevent retaliation against Muslims living in the US, especially after 9/11, many politicians, including Barack Obama, Hillary Clinton, and George W. Bush declared that Islam is a religion of peace. Nothing could be further from the truth. The Koran, written in reality by Mohammad, promulgates jihad. Jihad, which refers to a holy war waged on behalf of Islam as a religious duty, involves the forcible conversion of everyone on the planet to Islam. All those who are not of the Muslim faith are considered infidels. If these infidels do not convert, they must be killed or enslaved. Mohammad himself was a cold-blooded mass murderer.[30, 31, 32]

---

28 Zmirak and Perrotta, *Immigration*, p. 99.

29 Newt Gingrich, "Deport every Muslim who believes in Sharia," *Fox News*, Jul. 14, 2016, 9:18, https://www.youtube.com/watch?v=SNtGGFJOmYs.

30 Robert Spencer, *The Truth About Muhammad.*

31 Former CIA covert officer Bryan Dean Wright, "Stop calling Islam a 'religion of peace'," *Fox News*, Jun. 17, 2016, 4:00, https://www.youtube.com/watch?v=zmNdt-7CMjU.

32 Sam Harris, "Islam Is Not a Religion of Peace," *FORA.tv*, Dec. 30, 2010, 4:39, https://www.youtube.com/watch?v=LfKLV6rmLxE.

It is true that most Muslims are not terrorists, but most terrorism today is perpetrated by Muslims. The more obedient a Muslim becomes to the original teachings of Islam as taught in the Koran, the more violent that Muslim tends to become. Only wishy-washy Muslims lean toward peace.

Slogan 46: "Those undocumented migrants are dreamers."

Dreamers is a euphemistic term that falsely describes illegal immigrants. The Democrats and other liberals want to give amnesty to all those who profit from chain migration. Why? Because, as the Democrats claim, they are decent human beings who just want a better life. But the problem is, these dreamers mirror the backward civilizations they come from, nations with ethical and moral standards inferior to American standards.

Zmirak and Perrotta give the real reason why Democrats want illegals to be amnestied by DACA:

> What's more, the new arrivals overwhelmingly tend to vote liberal and pro-choice. The millions of future Democrats that "Dreamer" illegals amnestied by DACA could invite here in future decades would make their mark. They'd seal the fate of the Republican Party nationally. They'd turn states like Texas purple, then blue. We might never have another pro-life president again.[33]

Slogan 47: "You are sexist."

Progressives use this insult against men or women as another favorite go-to technique, similar to calling others racist. Feminists are especially guilty of playing the sex card.

Slogan 48: "You're a conspiracy theorist."

A conspiracy is a secret compact between two or more people to

---

33 Zmirak and Perrota, *Immigration*, p. 73.

engage in nefarious actions that bring the conspirators great rewards, usually wealth, influence, and power. However, these actions are always illegal, immoral, or fraudulent—that's why they are kept secret. Their actions can harm individuals, groups, and even entire nations.

Leftists employ the term conspiracy theorist to describe anyone who tries to uncover their devious plots against freedom. Today many people claim that their political opponents are relying on conspiracy theories. Most of these claims seem to be frivolous and just ploys to avoid real arguments. However, conspiracies are not always just theories but are frequently factual. That means conspiracies may not be just a theory, but a fact of history. I am a conspiracy analyst and investigator, not a conspiracy theorist.

Slogan 49: "You're a crazy truther."

The Left applies the word truther to anyone who believes in the reality of conspiracies. Leftists also call such people nutjobs, cultists, village idiots, and many other endearing epithets. What it all boils down to is that the Left wants to discourage any serious investigations into a large number of unusual and unexplained disasters like the attack of September 11, 2001 or the Sandy Hook Elementary School shooting on December 14, 2012. One of the basic purposes of these conspiracy deniers seems to be to eventually confiscate all guns owned by American citizens and to legally silence anyone who dares question the official versions of the facts.

The idea of truther is especially ironic since the liberal fake news outlets like CNN and MSNBC traffic in endless made-up conspiracies.

Slogan 50: "We stand for equality and social and economic justice."

Like all liberal buzz phrases, this sounds great! What could be more noble than social and economic justice? Shouldn't we all want it? But to a progressive "social and economic justice" means the reordering all of society in the image of their imaginary fantasy world and redistributing wealth to give the "disadvantaged" special privileges to the detriment of the "advantaged." And who are the advantaged? Usually they are people who work for a living and improve their condition by hard work, improved education, and personal ingenuity.

The demand for equality is a sacred progressive mantra. It is illogical and impossible to achieve. In nature and in the real world, absolute equality has never existed and never will. Only equality under the law is possible, although difficult to attain. This liberal demand boils down to socialism, where the strong central government steals wealth from the Haves and gives it to the Have Nots. It destroys the incentives of the Haves to work harder and to contribute more to society because if they do so, the government will confiscate more of the fruits of their labor.

It also destroys the incentives of the poor because if they can get what they want without working for it, then why should they take the trouble of improving their condition? The result of socialism will be, sooner or later, that all classes of people will be equally impoverished and miserable.

Slogan 51: "We fight for the common good, human compassion, compromise, positive change, and open-mindedness."

By expressing these noble claims ad infinitum, liberals exalt their superiority over everybody else. It implies that only *they* want these things. But what they really fight for is socialism, government control, the loss of individual freedom, and every destructive thing that most mainstream Americans oppose.

Slogan 52: "We must make the rich pay their fair share."

This injunction targets the "rich," whom the Left sees as greedy criminals. A wide range of opinions exist on this subject, and most of them are wrong. For example, one "tax expert" makes the claim that the rich in our country have inherited their wealth and did not work for it. That is false. So to obtain an honest appraisal of this problem, I depend on the judgment of PragerU, a source that I trust. UCLA economics professor, Lee Ohanian, makes the following analysis for PragerU:

- The top 10% of the population are considered reasonably well off. They earn at least $50,000 per year before deductions and taxes. But they pay 71% of all taxes collected while earning only 43% of all income. Fairness would suggest they should pay 43% in taxes, and thus they are paying more than their fair share.
- The top 5% of the population are considered very well off. They earn at least $190,000 before deductions and taxes.
- The top 1%, of the population are regarded as being rich. They make at least $500,000 before deductions and taxes, yet they pay 37% of all taxes paid in the country while earning only 17% of all income. To do this they must work very hard, take grave risks, and usually incur serious debt. Fairness would suggest they should pay 17% in taxes.
- The lower end, people making $45,000 or less (47% of all earners) pay little or no taxes.[34]

Our current progressive income tax system is already unfair, and to tax the rich even more would be immoral and counterproductive. It would be counterproductive because the higher the taxes, the more investment and risk-taking decline, resulting in fewer good jobs for average Americans and greater suffering for the poor. It is a tyrannical system that forces most wage-earning Americans to pay close to 60% of their income to the big spenders in Washington and local governments. We should dump the current system and replace it with the Flat Tax or the Fair Tax. One of the greatest benefits of this change would be to rid ourselves of the IRS.

---

34 PragerU, "Do the Rich Pay Their Fair Share?" Feb. 16, 2015, 5:13, https://www.youtube.com/watch?v=DnEe4oaSC88.

Slogan 53: "Felons are justice-involved individuals, juvenile delinquents are effected by the justice system, and drug addicts are impacted by substance use."

These are some of the friendly and kind euphemisms developed by the Democrat leaders of San Francisco to hide the terrible crime problems in their city. Instead of working to resolve these problems, the leaders use fancy terms to excuse themselves from taking meaningful action. Note that felons are not called criminals, which they are, but justice-involved people. Note also that drug addicts "use" dangerous substances, kind of like people with diabetes who "use" pharmaceuticals. This draws moral equivalence between legitimate drug use and illegitimate substance "abuse." All this is typical of progressives using tricky language to confuse the issues.[35]

Slogan 54: "Both the Left and the Right engage in ugly hostility."

This claim is a feeble effort to justify the habitual violent behavior of leftists: "They all do it, so no one has a right to complain!" It is a complete falsehood. Yes, there are times when right-wing whack jobs get carried away, and there is no justification for that, yet those events are rare. But there is no moral equivalence here. Nearly all the violence, intimidation, anger, and outright hatred come from radical liberals.

There are no conservatives who engage in the violent behavior of the Communists who laughingly call themselves "Antifa."

Rita Panahi of Sky News Australia said that blaming current ugly hostility on both sides is "a falsehood that must not go unchallenged." She continues by adding:

> Pretending that both the left and the right are equally culpable is not a nuanced view, it is demonstrably

35 Tucker Carlson, "Those who control your words control your mind," *Fox News*, Aug. 22, 2019, 3:46, https://www.youtube.com/watch?v=PFydGLt79y4.

> false . . . The left-leaning speakers do not require riot squads to keep protestors away and are not presented with massive bills from police for being victims of violent activists. Mainstream conservatives are subjected to unhinged activists who feel entitled to bully and intimidate not only them but their audience.[36, 37]

Bernie Sanders also habitually wallows in the false concept of moral equivalence when he compares socialist and Communist countries to America with its capitalism.[38]

Slogan 55: "We developed the adversity score."

Recently, the College Entrance Examination Board adopted the "adversity score" to modify scores on the SAT exam. Those who are poor, black, Muslim, or disadvantaged in any way receive added points on the SAT in order to give them a "just" advantage in being accepted into colleges. This means that the adversity score is another form of reverse racism and sexism, just like affirmative action. An uproar from parents forced the College Board to drop this discriminatory scoring.[39]

Slogan 56: "She is woke."

Concerning this slogan, an article in Conservapedia quotes the token conservative David Brooks of the New York Times as saying:

---

36 Rita Panahi, "To blame both sides for 'ugly hostility' is 'a falsehood'," *Sky News Australia*, 10/10/2019, 5:51, https://www.skynews.com.au/details/_6093913640001.

37 Casselman and Daughtry, *Waking the Sleeping Giant*, pp. 60-63.

38 Laura Ingraham on The Angle with Dinesh D'Souza, "Sanders is a product of academic nostrums taking over mainstream culture," *Fox News*, Feb. 26, 2020, 3:42, esp. 2:50, https://www.youtube.com/watch?v=wx24N-hriYw.

39 Liz Wheeler on Tipping Point, "SAT Removes 'Woke' Adversity Score," *One America News Network*, Aug. 28, 2019, 3:22, https://www.youtube.com/watch?v=pKcWcxLfyqI.

> To be woke is to be radically aware and justifiably paranoid. It is to be cognizant of the rot pervading the power structures. The woke manner shares cool's rebel posture, but it is the opposite of cool in certain respects. Cool was politically detached, but being a social activist is required for being woke. Cool was individualistic, but woke is nationalistic and collectivist. Cool was emotionally reserved; woke is angry, passionate and indignant. Cool was morally ambiguous; woke seeks to establish a clear marker for what is unacceptable.[40]

David Brooks is wrong here on most accounts. Wokeness is not a good thing. It is to be hypersensitive and paranoid without justification. It is to grossly exaggerate the supposed "rot" in American society. Being a social activist is not required to be woke, but blindly and gullibly following and parroting the leftist paradigms *is* required. Wokeness is not nationalist but rather collectivist, which is the opposite of nationalist. The boundaries wokeness creates are determined solely by emotion and subjective relativism.

In other words, woke means to be awake or fully aware of the injustices in life. Anyone who sees the real problems in our society is said to be woke by the Left. The problem is that these fully awakened people tend to see the world only through the biases of the Left and thus they see no good but only bad. Actually, the use of woke is a rallying call of the Left to incite people to take action.

Slogan 57: "We must put people before profits."

This is another hypocritical liberal catchphrase. It is a disguised, or not so disguised, attack on free enterprise capitalism. Without profits no business could survive, and without businesses the people would not have jobs, food, homes, etc.

---

40 Brooks, David. "How Cool Works in America Today," *New York Times*, July 25, 2017, accessed on Feb 14, 2018.

Slogan 58: "Peoplekind, not mankind."

This is a term used by progressives to replace "mankind," which they see as discriminatory against women. The Left is always hard at work trying to tear down all the traditions of Western Society, and that is often done through the manipulation of language. Recently, Justin Trudeau, prime minister of Canada, corrected a woman's question during a town hall meeting. In her question she used the word "mankind," and Trudeau smugly insisted that now we should all use "peoplekind" instead.[41]

Slogan 59: "We are tolerant. You are not."

Progressives insist endlessly that they are tolerant, but they are only tolerant of themselves, their fellow travelers, their own ideals and opinions. For instance, progressives hate Christianity, and in all their speeches, writings, and meetings they view conservative, Bible-believing Christians as persona non grata. They are extremely intolerant concerning Christianity because of its insistence upon personal responsibility and moral absolutes.

Progressives know that a society without moral absolutes and a belief in personal responsibility will eventually fall prey to the Left's greed and lust to rule. Why? Because people displaying self-reliance and rugged individualism are also people who think for themselves.

Nevertheless, progressives are eminently tolerant in one way. They are tolerant of evil, lies, violence, and disruption. In other terms, liberals are not liberal.

Slogan 60: "Marriage and family are outdated because they are patriarchal institutions that oppress women and children."

Liberals solemnly declare that they despise marriage and family because they are oppressive, but the real reason they despise those

41 *CTV News*, "Trudeau tells woman to say 'peoplekind' not 'mankind,'" Feb. 7, 2018, :49, https://www.youtube.com/watch?v=Uln6ULsPQno.

institutions is because they reject sexual promiscuity, thus undermining one of the principal supports of liberalism.

Slogan 61: "To save lives we must outlaw all assault weapons, weapons of war, and machine guns."

In the liberal mindset, all firearms, especially "big guns," are assault weapons and weapons of war. The hard core leftists know this is not true, but they promote the idea anyway to further their ultimate goal of total gun confiscation.

Liberals call all semiautomatic rifles weapons of war, especially those that look scary to them. For example, the AR-15 is just a semiautomatic rifle no matter what it looks like, but liberals shudder in horror when they mention it. An AR-15 is not nearly as powerful as a 30-06, a rifle used for hunting, which is also semiautomatic. Often they confuse semiautomatic weapons with machine guns, which are fully automatic.

The purchase of machine guns has been against the law since 1986. With a machine gun you pull the trigger and the rounds fire rapidly until you release the trigger. With a semiautomatic rifle, you must pull the trigger each time you want to fire a round. Semiautomatic rifles are not weapons of war.

In line with their agenda, liberals conveniently pass over the fact that most firearm crime is done with handguns, not rifles.

In his crusade against guns, Ralph Northam, the Democrat governor of Virginia, proposed draconian laws in January of 2020 to deprive the citizens of that state of their Second Amendment rights. This developed especially after a nutjob, DeWayne Craddock, shot and killed twelve people in Virginia City in May, 2019.

Every time some maniac shoots people with a gun, the gun grabbers stand on the graves of the victims to promote their agenda. They just cannot seem to understand or admit that sick, deranged people do the killing, not the guns. Either that, or they purposely refuse to understand it.

Fortunately, there's a new movement to combat the state gun grabbers. A large number of municipalities and counties have set up Second Amendment sanctuaries, and this movement is growing.

Slogan 62: "But . . . but guns kill people."

Guns do not kill people. Bad people use guns and a multitude of other weapons to kill people. Moreover, automobiles, knives, saws, pencils, and many other tools can injure or kill people if they are used to do harm. Should we ban all these things? Of course not. This simple fact seems beyond the grasp of most liberals and gun grabbers.

Slogan 63: "We must pass safe, responsible, common-sense gun-control laws."

When Democrats talk about common sense gun laws, they are talking about zero common sense. They really mean gun control according to their desires. They have been chipping away at the Second Amendment for decades and will not stop until it becomes completely meaningless. And when the Second Amendment is undermined, the first, fourth, fifth, and sixth amendments are gone too. That's when the central government bent on total control can disarm all Americans and eventually establish a tyrannical government like that of Venezuela.[42]

Some liberals claim that it would be useless for Americans to be armed because they could never match the firepower of the government. If this is true, why then did Nazi Germany and Communist dictators make sure their subjects were first disarmed before they began to establish their dictatorships? No government, no matter how powerful, can overcome a well-armed citizenry.

The gun grabbers just can't get it through their thick skulls

---

42 Graham Ledger on The Daily Ledger, "Lynchburg, VA City Councilman, Jeff Helgeson, on Protecting Gun Rights," *One America News Network*, Jan. 16, 2020, 5:49, https://www.youtube.com/watch?v=rg_sV9YAoew.

that guns do not kill anyone. The killing is done by sick maniacs and bad people.

Slogan 64: "You don't need an AR-15."

In their effort to get rid of all guns, leftists constantly assert what we do need and what we do not need. There are many reasons why people might want to buy an AR-15 and use magazines in excess of ten rounds, but we do not need to explain that. Instead, we should go on the offensive by saying, "Who are you to decide what I need? Who made you God?"

As Liz Wheeler says, "It's not the bill of needs; it's the Bill of Rights."[43]

While debating guns with Ben Shapiro, Piers Morgan, CNN analyst, said, "What I haven't heard is one coherent reason why any civilian in America needs an AR-15, military-style assault weapon. Tell me why you need one." Shapiro replied that the Founding Fathers wrote the Second Amendment to protect Americans from potential government tyranny.[44]

That is a good answer but, in addition, Piers Morgan should be reminded that Americans are not obligated to justify their need for a weapon like the AR-15.

Slogan 65: "Trump is a fearmonger."

Yes, Trump is a fearmonger to liberals because he opposes much of their agenda. They base this claim to a large extent on some of Trump's silly tweets and not on what he actually does.

Slogan 66: "Republicans always engage in negative campaigning."

This is the hilarious slogan the Left uses to characterize any

---

43 Liz Wheeler on Tipping Point, "Pregnant Lady Uses AR-15 to Kill Intruder," *OAN,* Nov. 4, 2019, 2:49, https://www.youtube.com/watch?v=3ZKKofrFQuc.

44 Live CNN, "Ben Shapiro and Piers Morgan on guns," *CNN*, Jan. 13, 2013, 4:31, https://www.youtube.com/watch?v=wRyT-45vFzk.

campaign tactic or slogan they do not like or cannot counteract effectively and logically. Democrats and other liberals are notorious for using negative campaigning far more than Republicans.

Slogan 67: "That's not socialism done right, or it's not pure socialism."

This concept is used to defend and promote socialism. If conservative critics point to certain socialist countries, such as Venezuela, and blame socialism for causing disruption, riots, protests, scarcities, poverty, and government tyranny, the defenders of socialism will often claim that the socialist principle was not "done right" in that country.

The obvious problem with this claim is that there is no right or wrong socialism. Every variety of socialism is still just socialism no matter what clever spin is put on it.

Slogan 68: "We must pass this legislation for the greater good."

The idea of doing something for the greater good is a typical leftist mantra to justify destructive policies that the Left promotes. The problem with it is that if the majority receives a good or a benefit and the minority does not, then the minority will be disenfranchised and injured. The Bill of Rights was adopted to protect the minority from losing its God-given, natural rights. If a person chooses to sacrifice himself for the greater good, that is an exercise in freedom. But when the government mandates what is for the greater good, that is tyranny. Many jurisdictions and most schools mandate vaccines for the alleged greater good.

Slogan 69: "That's evil because it's cultural appropriation."

Liberals who say that no one has the right to mimic or enjoy aspects of foreign cultures are speaking nonsense. Their real goal is to tear down American traditions. But the people who scream "cultural appropriation" have no authority whatsoever.

American cultural practices have their origins in many foreign cultures, in immensely complex ways. But of course, the only cultures the leftists are concerned about are the *persecuted* cultures of "people of color," usually meaning blacks, Hispanics, and Muslims. No other cultures count. In truth, these "cultural appropriations" are a sign of appreciation and a tribute to the cultures that originated them. We must remember that America is a melting pot of multiple cultures.[45]

Slogan 70: "This is stolen land."

This refers to the concept that when Anglos migrated to America, they conquered the indigenous peoples, the American Indians, and stole their lands. As a result of this, the Left insists that whites should feel terribly guilty forever and ever and also pay severe reparations.

The problem with this idea is that these events happened hundreds of years ago. Present-day whites are innocent of what their ancestors did, and the Indians of today are not the victims of the past. Therefore, whites should not be punished and Indians rewarded. The job of who should receive reparations, who should pay them, and how they should be paid is virtually impossible to determine. The same is true of the reparations demanded by the Left for blacks.

Moreover, history reveals that all lands across the planet have been "stolen" at some point in time because the number of migrations, invasions, occupations, and conquests have been huge and occurred over a period of thousands of years.

In the case of the North American Indians, nearly all the tribes engaged in continuous wars for territory and resources. As one tribe gained in population and power, they typically invaded and seized the lands of weaker tribes. Later, that same land was overrun by still other tribes. Should we enlist the services of hundreds of

45 Lauren Southern, "Cultural appropriation isn't racist—It's really cultural appreciation," *Rebel News*, Sept. 21, 2015, 6:29, https://www.youtube.com/watch?v=VwQvnyIR90.

computers and "experts" to determine which tribes were deprived and should receive reparations, which tribes should pay them, and how much should be paid?

All this reparations nonsense is nothing but a fluffy effort of the Left to malign Anglos and delegitimize the American nation.

Slogan 71: "You must be a liberal or a leftist."

Leftists adore reading opponents' minds and falsely labeling them. They seem oblivious to the fact that we should judge people by their consistent actions, not by some imaginary attributes. The Left has no problem using self-projection by calling conservatives "leftists, liberals, fascists, Nazis, deseasers, bullies, haters," and so forth. Labels are good if they are accurate, but they are bad if they are not accurate. I just remind these lefties that insults are not arguments. Conservatives do not have to try to read the minds of the Left: their words and actions reveal their real intent.

Slogan 72: "Well, she didn't deny it."

When Hillary Clinton accused Tulsi Gabbard of being groomed by the Russians, an MSNBC reporter solemnly declared, "Well, she didn't deny it," and her fellow reporters applauded that idiotic statement. In other words, when Tulsi defended herself, she did not specifically deny being a Russian asset. Therefore, in leftist mentality, that is absolute proof that she *is* a Russian asset. That is typical of the kind of doublethink the Left wallows in.

We saw the same doublethink in the hearings on Brett Kavanaugh for justice of the Supreme Court. The Democrat inquisitors declared that since Kavanaugh could not prove he did not molest Christine Blasey Ford decades earlier, he must be guilty. In fact, Kavanaugh's detractors produced their own irrational slogan: "I believe her."

So, the just, time-honored, legal principle that the accused is innocent until proven guilty was completely turned upside down and ignored by the liberal questioners and the compliant media.

Slogan 73: "Whites and conservatives are guilty of microagressions."

Microaggression is a term used for brief and commonplace, daily verbal, behavioral, or environmental indignities, whether intentional or unintentional, that communicate hostile, derogatory, or negative prejudicial slights and insults toward any group, particularly culturally marginalized groups.[46]

The Left considers microaggression to be a serious form of racism against people of color. Consequently, they adore blaming whites for microaggressions toward any class of people they claim to protect, such as blacks, Hispanics, Muslims, and the LGBTQ. However, all these supposed microaggressions are based on subjective, emotional, and imaginary perceptions, and thus are not compelling.

The following reference satirically exposes the Left's foolish doctrine of microagression.[47]

Buzzfeed, a biased liberal news outlet, presents a number of alleged microagressions, supposedly proliferated by conservatives:

- "What are you?" (to a person of mixed ethnic heritage)
- "So what do you guys speak in Japan? Asian?"
- "You don't act like a normal black person, ya know."
- "Courtney, I never see you as a black girl."
- "Just because I'm Mexican doesn't mean I should be chosen as 'Dora the Explorer' in the high school skit."
- "So, like, what are you?" (to a person of color)
- "You don't speak Spanish?" (to a Mexican girl)
- "No, you're white." (to a white girl)
- "When people think it's weird when I listen to Carry Underwood." (to a black girl)
- "This girl sitting next to me moves, to sit closer to someone

46 Wikipedia.

47 Lou Perez, "How to Stop Microaggressions," *We the Internet TV*, Sept. 16, 2016, 3:38, https://www.youtube.com/watch?v=tqnqolO2FTk.

she's talking to, and this white guy whispers loudly that she moved because 'I smell like rice.'" (to an Asian girl)
- "So . . . you're Chinese . . . right?" (to a Chinese girl)[48]

Some of these comments do seem clumsy and perhaps culturally insensitive, but only a person who needs to be psychologically coddled would be profoundly offended by any of them.

Slogan 74: "We can't support an alt-right candidate."

Alt-right is a term the Left uses to ridicule and discredit conservatives and their beliefs. After reading the definitions of alt-right in standard dictionaries like Webster's, Cambridge, Oxford, and Collins, and rejecting leftists sources like Wikipedia, Vox, and the New York Times, I chose the online Conservapedia as giving the most complete and honest definition of alt-right:

> The term "alt-right" has more than one definition, and this article currently uses both. The alt-right, or alternative right, is an emerging faction of the right-wing that opposes unrestrained multiculturalism, un-"skilled" immigration, and globalization. The alt-right has emerged as one of the central opponents of the Establishment. Although originally intended to refer to nationalist and anti-establishment conservatives, liberals have twisted the term and have used it to describe white supremacists and neo-Nazis. Regardless of the definition(s) of "alt-right," the Left's extreme beliefs and behaviors are the cause of the alt-right's growth, not conservatives. The alt-right movement's central theme is as follows: The alt-right is not defined by any particular school of thought, but by the neoliberal school

48 Heben Nigatu, "21 Racial Microaggressions You Hear on a Daily Basis," *BuzzFeed*, Dec. 9, 2013, https://www.buzzfeed.com/hnigatu/racial-microagressions-you-hear-on-a-daily-basis.

> of thought it rejects. The alt-right, in the simplest terms, is an unapologetic purging of liberal idiocy.

So the Left twisted the term to mean something it did not originally mean and instead turned into something ugly. The term Alternative Right was first popularized in 2010 by Richard Spencer and Colin Liddell and was then a positive force, but as time progressed, Richard Spencer, the American neo-Nazi and white supremacist, broke away from the movement and went his way. Colin Liddell and others then changed the name of the online site from Alternative Right to the more positive Affirmative Right.[49]

Slogan 75: "We are conservatives too."

Some liberal groups try to pass themselves off as conservatives because conservatism has gained a better reputation than liberalism, and leftists know it. In this way they can continue to preach liberal doctrines under the safer patina of conservatism, hoping at the same time to confuse some genuine conservatives as to what they believe or should believe.

For example, *The New American* magazine says:

> The *Weekly Standard*, a magazine that had been described as a "redoubt of neoconservatism" and as "the neocon bible," published its final issue on December 17 [2018], 23 years after being founded by veteran neoconservative William Kristol. Though practically all media reports (including the *New York Times, The Hill, CNN,* and the *Washington Post*) described the *Weekly Standard* as "conservative," such descriptions are merely reflections of how the term "conservative" has been corrupted in recent years.[50]

---

49 Colin Liddell, "The End of the Alt-Right: Colin Liddell Interviewed by Quebec Nationalist Magazine 'Harfang'," *Affirmative Right*, Aug. 2018, https://affirmativeright.blogspot.com/2018/08/the-end-of-alt-right-colin-liddell.html.

50 *The New American*, p. 8, Jan. 21, 2019.

Conservapedia defines a neoconservative as "someone presented as a 'conservative' but who actually favors big government, globalism, interventionism, perpetual war, and a hostility to religion in politics and government. The word means 'newly conservative,' and thus formerly liberal." In other words, a neocon is a liberal in disguise.

Slogan 76: "You can't legislate morality."

This slogan is a favorite of the Left. It may be true that if we lived in a perfect world of angels, we would need no laws other than the self-imposed rules of our own God-given conscience. Man-made laws cannot make us moral people if our tendencies lean toward immoral behavior. And if we embrace moral relativism, we have no guiding light to help us understand right from wrong, and in that case, no laws can transform our being toward the good.

However, good laws can force us to *behave* like moral people. In fact, that's the primary purpose of most laws. The more we behave as moral people, the fewer legal restraints are necessary. But the less morality we exhibit, the more it is necessary to increase the number of laws.

The Founding Fathers understood this; that's why they wrote the Bill of Rights, to control the natural tendency of leaders, in this case federal leaders, to abuse their power.

John Adams, second president of the US, said, "Our Constitution was made only for a moral and religious people. It is wholly inadequate to the government of any other."

As John Emerich Edward Dalberg Acton said, "Power tends to corrupt and absolute power corrupts absolutely. Great men are almost always bad men."

In our everyday lives, we see people willfully engaging in destructive behavior: exceeding the speed limits, cheating in business deals, scamming innocent people, selling illegal drugs, stealing from stores, murdering people, and so forth. The responsibility to control and curtail such behavior normally lies with the states, who must make laws to deter and punish such behavior.

This does not mean that states or communities should have the right to make rules restricting your right to work by requiring licenses, to force you to get hunting or fishing licenses or any other kind of permits. All these things have nothing to do with morality and are nothing but abusive taxes that infringe on freedom.

One of the worst problems we face as Americans are the thousands of bureaucratic regulations which have the force of laws. They are "laws" which have nothing to do with morality and constantly interfere with our natural right of self-defense and to use our property as we feel fit. The unelected bureaucrats who make these regulations are power-mad and represent the greatest threat to liberty.

Slogan 77: "Stop! Stop! You're triggering me!"

Liberal wimps, wusses, sissies, and delicate, sensitive snowflakes hate it when someone upsets their comfortable cradle, so with great tears in their eyes they cry out, "Stop triggering me!" In other words, "I can't bear hearing the truth!"

Slogan 78: "You're hurting my feelings."

Many delicate, sensitive liberals are deeply offended simply because you disagree with them. This permits them to cry and whine and justifies them getting special privileges at the expense of everybody else.[51, 52]

Slogan 79: "They were underage women."

In the case of billionaire Jeffrey Epstein, who was found guilty of pedophilia, leftist news sources such as CNN called his victims

---

51 Dan Adamini, "Liberal Feelings," From the radio show In the Right Mind with Dam Adamini, *DJA RightMind*, Sept. 21, 2015, 4:07, https://www.youtube.com/watch?v=rnfreaK_SQo.

52 Ben Shapiro, "Facts Don't Care About Your Feelings," *PragerU*, May 11, 2017, 4:17, https://www.youtube.com/watch?v=Hok2PiRnDfw.

"underage women." But there is no such thing as underage women. They are either young women or children. Some of Epstein's victims were as young as fourteen. At any rate, it would also be evil if Epstein had seduced and manipulated women of any age.

The Left, in waging war against America, habitually represents gross evil as "not really all that bad." In the segment referenced below, the term "underage women"is used fifteen times in one minute.[53]

In 1977, film director Roman Polanski was found guilty of raping thirteen-year-old Samantha Gailey. Later, leftist Whoopi Goldberg claimed that it was not really "rape rape." This shows how the Left is willing to twist the meaning of words to explain away horrendous sexual abuse.[54]

Slogan 80: "I identify as a woman/man."

In their crusade to destroy America, the traditional family, and decent morality, liberals reject binary relationships (you are either male or female) and claim that there are multiple, legitimate gender identities, perhaps even an infinite number of them. That means that if a grown man who was born with normal male sexual parts decides he feels, imagines, or aspires to be a woman, or even a female child, then he is indeed that. And anyone who challenges his new identity is a hateful, sexist, despicable person.

In other words, the Left in their infinite kindness and super sensitivity do not want to offend any poor suffering soul. No, not anyone. Except the untold number of people whose lives are destroyed by such an insane doctrine.

As a result of this foolishness, transgender males demand the legal right to use women's restrooms and locker rooms no matter how much that offends the modesty of the women. And also, they

---

53 Jezebel, "Stop Calling Epstein's Alleged Victims 'Underage Women,'" July 12, 2019, 1:06, https://www.youtube.com/watch?v=cb5o9B3lTOM.

54 Bob Enyart, "Whoopi Goldberg: Polanski Child Rape Wasn't Real Rape," June 17, 2015, 3:04, https://www.youtube.com/watch?v=sHflBPU-DtA.

demand the right to compete unfairly in women's sports, thus depriving many young women of potential scholarships and the joy of receiving merited accolades because of their dedicated training.

The saddest part of this is the many school districts, city councils, liberal leaders, and women's sport authorities who cave in to the "desperate needs" of this weird, mentally ill minority, supported of course by the liberal media. The following reference satirizes the transgender gospel.[55]

Slogan 81: "Donald Trump is an existential threat."

And all this time, I thought global warming was supposed to be the great existential threat! The media, the Democrats, and all Trump's detractors repeat ad infinitum the ridiculous, unsubstantiated claim that the president is an existential threat. This vague, abstract wording is used purposely because it sounds horrible but conveniently makes no specific claims that can be easily refuted. By contrast, Trump, in his debates with Hillary Clinton, used more concrete language when he said, "If elected president, Hillary will destroy America."

Slogan 82: "We live in a rape culture."

This is a favorite theme of radical feminists who want to vilify American culture. However, this claim is so vague and abstract that it is impossible to disprove, and the feminists know that. Conservatives should expose those facts and then demand that the feminists give real, specific examples that can be logically addressed and fought.

In the following video, we are brought to a feminist event, a group march to propagandize feminist views. Conservative analyst Lauren Southern interviews a feminist who is "proving her point"

---

55 Joseph Backholm, "The Binary That Really Needs to Go Away," *Family Policy Institute of Washington,* Jan. 2, 2018, 3:43, https://www.youtube.com/watch?v=u_WNRo8Jl74.

somehow by walking down the sidewalk half naked. I assume she is trying to say that women have a right to wear whatever they want or nothing at all, and men alone have the burden of controlling every urge to sexually approach them. Thus, the burden of decency is placed fully on the shoulders of men, and people have no right to expect women to contribute to social morality.[56, 57]

Slogan 83: "We should be investing in our country and redistributing wealth and power in our society for the benefit of all."

This high-sounding rhetoric about investing and redistributing wealth boils down to nothing more than a plea for socialism. So, the Left will use the government to confiscate your income and give it to the poor.[58]

Slogan 84: "We are pragmatists, realists, empiricists, and care only about facts."

Unlike conservatives, liberals claim not to hold to any ideology when they make a ridiculous ideological argument. As Jonah Goldberg says, "They hide ideological claims in rhetorical Trojan horses, hoping to conquer terrain unearned by real debate." Five of their clichés are

- diversity is strength,
- violence never solved anything,
- the living Constitution,
- Social Darwinism, and

---

56 Lauren Southern, "Lauren Southern clashes with feminists at SlutWalk," *Rebel Media*, June 9, 2015, 3:43, https://www.youtube.com/watch?v=7QvswaYWL0.

57 Steven Crowder, "Crazy SJW Girl FREAKS OUT on Rape Culture | Louder With Crowder," *CrowderBits,* March 7, 2020, https://www.youtube.com/watch?v=HqIblDLzY0.

58 Mike Huckabee, "Huckabee on Johnson victory, says Trump will be elected in a 'landslide'," *Fox News,* Dec. 13, 2019, 5:23, https://www.youtube.com/watch?v=_rMapoWwf40.

- better ten guilty men go free.[59] (But everyone already knows this, so it is not an argument.)

In reality, liberals depend solely on feelings, emotions, and unsupported opinions and generally reject empiricism, pragmatism, and facts.

Slogan 85: "We fact-checked this."

Democrats and other liberals love to claim that your statements are false and theirs are true because they have fact-checked them. For that reason, we are obligated to admit we are wrong. In reality, they have not fact-checked anything but only repeat the same fake factoids they have been promulgating for years. While doing this, they try to enhance the validity of their claims by consulting a written document on which they have recorded their "facts."

Candy Crowley, CNN anchor, pulled this trick on Mitt Romney during his second presidential debate with Barack Obama.[60]

Slogan 86: "We need health care reform."

This is LeftSpeak for we need "health care takeover" by the government.[61]

Slogan 87: "We must pass this important stimulus bill."

This is LeftSpeak for we must pass this "controversial bailout."[62]

---

59 Jonah Goldberg, "Top Five Clichés Liberals Use To Avoid Real Arguments," *Washington Post*, April 27, 2012, text, https://www.washingtonpost.com/opinions/top-five-cliches-liberals-use-to-avoid-real-arguments/2012/04/27/gIQAFR1zlT_story.html.

60 "Raw Video: Second Obama - Romney presidential debate," *CNN*, Oct. 17, 2012, 1:37:48, esp. 1:14:55, https://www.youtube.com/watch?v=4BTk2bKJ6uI.

61 Casselman and Daughtry, *Waking the Sleeping Giant*, p. 37.

62 Casselman and Daughtry, *Waking the Sleeping Giant*, p. 37.

Slogan 88: "Clarence Thomas is not black enough."

Leftists savaged Supreme Court Justice Clarence Thomas, a black man, by calling him "not black enough" when he ruled against one of their cherished projects supposedly supporting blacks.[63]

Slogan 89: "Our treasured words are justice, truth, equality, fairness, tolerance, love, kindness, peace, common sense, good, polite, noble, incorruptible, virtuous, blameless, high-minded, open-minded, moral, powerful, dedicated, righteous, high-roaders, decent, great, and so forth."

These are wonderful words, aren't they? When used in normal parlance, they describe someone or something of great value, don't they? Absolutely! But in the mouths of Democrats and other liberals, they become verbal traps to deceive, manipulate, and exploit the unwary. When leftists use such terms, they almost always mean exactly the opposite of what the term normally means. This is because leftists are masters of the bluff and the Big Lie.

This tactic of people setting themselves up as people of virtue is predicted in 2 Corinthians 11:14-15, where Satan transforms himself as an angel of light and his followers as ministers of righteousness.

---

63 Casselman and Daughtry, *Waking the Sleeping Giant*, p. 49, citing *Newsmax.com*, November 1, 2005.

CHAPTER FOUR

Primary Tactics of the Left: Deceptive Content

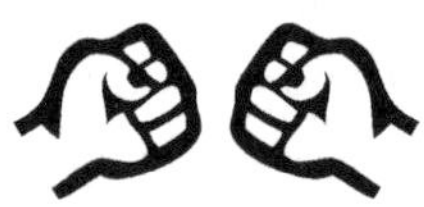

These tactics, which I call "strategies," comprise several types: intellectual deception, bullying, and calls for violence.

Strategy 1: outright lying

It is often difficult to tell whether or not your opponent is telling the truth, but there are certain signs that suggest he or she may be lying:

1. Follow the money. Is the arguer receiving funds, benefits, grants, or any other type of remuneration for his stance?
2. Follow the celebrity. Does the arguer depend on the opinion of celebrities, who normally know no more than ordinary citizens? It is different if the celebrity has special knowledge or experience, but the Left's use of paid celebrities is not justified because that represents a conflict of interest.
3. Follow the profane. If an arguer uses vulgar language, swearing, insults, cheap shots, is overbearing, condescending, or pretentious, that suggests he is lying because he depends

on unfair tactics of argumentation. Unfortunately, some decent and honest people also fall into the same trap.

4. Recognize the lies. Liberals often provide information that is self-evidently false, information that any intelligent person with common sense would reject.
5. Follow the sources. Liberals frequently rely on the prejudiced mainstream media for their ideas and "facts," and they parrot those duplicitous ideas without critical thinking. Or they depend on known biased subversives. In this case they are repeating lies knowingly or unwittingly.[64]

Strategy 2: conflating opinions with facts

What follows is a real-life discussion on social media between an atheist, obviously a progressive, debating with a believer.

Subject: The existence of God
Actors: Robert (L), William (C)

Robert: I feel as humans, or peoplekind if you prefer, we need to end the practice of all religions. Its 2018. Its time to trade magic for fact . . . no trade backs.

William: I disagree with you.

Robert: It does more harm than good and is ALL MAN MADE MAKE BELIEVE!

William: I disagree with you.

Robert: We are not special. We are born we live and we die and that's it. That's all you get like it or not. I for one am fine with just having gotten the chance to exist and can come to terms with the fact that one day I will be gone and I'm okay with that. I don't need any b******* promise of an afterlife to keep me comfortable

---

64 John Stossel, "The Lie of the Left," *LibertyPen,* Aug. 18, 2015, 4:44, https://www.youtube.com/watch?v=O_CH3w5SxDc.

during this life and to keep me free of fear I don't have any fear I get to live and one day I will die and that's it.

William: You're entitled to your opinion, but it's just an opinion.

Robert: Except that it's not just an opinion. There has never been any God. We as humans do not require religion to do good in this life and to be the best we can be in this life. The fact that science is coming as far as it has to the point where we can create human life if we so choose to should be enough to prove that there is no God because if there really was I'm sure that he slashed she would not allow us to do so. There has never been and never will be any evidence that God exists or that an afterlife exists.

William: You are simply repeating the same opinions over and over. Your opinions are not facts. I respect your right to have those opinions, but I disagree with them.

Robert punched Like on this last comment. He seems to be sincere, but we must remember that when a leftist uses the words "good" and "best" they often have special meanings for those terms. These are Robert's so-called facts:

- We can just "end" all religions.
- Religion mostly does harm and is make-believe.
- We are not special.
- The idea of an afterlife is only meant to assuage fear.
- There never has been a God.
- Science can now create life, so this proves there is no God.
- [The nonexistent] God would not allow us to create life (like through procreation?).
- My statements are facts, not just opinion.

Robert's excessive, emotional insistence that God does not exist leads us to believe he really wishes someone could prove him wrong. The only reasonable thing he actually says is that people do not need religion to do good and be good. The problem is, it is much more difficult for people to do good without spiritual guidance.

William seems to realize that the question of whether God exists or not is an immensely complex issue and not easy to discuss on social media. He recognizes that Robert is a trickle-down liberal when he uses "peoplekind," a term popularized by progressive Canadian prime minister, Justin Trudeau.[65] William sees that Robert is unlikely to change his ideas easily, so he does not even try.

Strategy 3: double-talk, doublespeak, and doublethink

- Webster's on double-talk: language that appears to be earnest and meaningful but in fact is a mixture of sense and nonsense; inflated, involved, and often deliberately ambiguous language.
- Webster's on doublespeak: language used to deceive usually through concealment or misrepresentation of truth.
- Webster's on doublethink: a simultaneous belief in two contradictory ideas.

A liberal made this comment on social media: "I did not say you were closed-mind. You are only closed-minded if you OWN that characterization. You only think it's a personal attack if you own it."

This is, of course, nonsense. The facts reveal if you are closed- or open-minded regardless of what you think about it. A personal attack is obviously a personal attack no matter how the progressive tries to spin it. This tactic is a form of moral relativism and justifies the user in making all the unfair, vicious attacks he desires.

What would the liberal say if the conservative turned the tables on him?

Conservative: Okay, let's see how you like it. You are a brain-dead, irrational, ignorant liberal.

---

65 "Trudeau corrects woman for using 'mankind' at town hall," *Fox News*, Feb. 6, 2018, https://www.youtube.com/watch?v=G-dPmFJ5IUk.

Now don't complain about those designations. They are only true if you own them.

In another example of nonsensical speech, a male caller on the Judge Jeanine Pirro show accuses her of being racist and despicable because she supposedly supports the persecution of people the caller claims are Mexican Americans living near the southern border. The judge replies, "I refuse to accept your recitation of the facts."

In the comment section, a commenter says, "The judge said, 'I refuse to accept your recitation of the facts,' so she just admitted that facts don't matter to her."

This critic misrepresents Pirro's statement: she rejects the caller's recitation of the facts, not the facts themselves. There are facts in this case, but the caller has made a selection from those facts, interpreted them according to his personal biases, and now presents his biases to Judge Jeanine in an effort to discredit her. The judge is better informed than the caller and knows the "real" facts and thus rejects his misrepresentations.[66]

Strategy 4: excessive emotion

Most leftist arguments are laced with great emotion. Here are some examples I've heard liberals use:

- "Oh, you're just lashing out."
- "You just hate everybody!"
- "Stop spreading hate!"
- "You're a terrible, mean bully." (cry, cry, sniff, sniff)
- "Hah! You're waving a fairy wand."
- "All you can use is fact after fact. It's so annoying."
- "You're not using enough facts."
- "You're acting like a big bully." (cry, cry, sniff, sniff)

---

66 "Fox News Host Jeanine Pirro Owned by On-Air Caller," *NowThis News*, Live TV, Sept. 16, 2019, 1:57, https://www.youtube.com/watch?v=G-0FaZNDhgA.

These emotional responses show that your liberal opponent has no facts to contribute to the discussion. People who scream, bawl, whine, cry, and rant with great anger, hate, and violence are nearly always wrong. And the more certain, dogmatic, and rigid they are in their opinions, the more certain it is that those opinions are false.

When progressives act this way, I usually answer, "What is your point" or "Why do you say that?" Or I avoid any further contact with them.

Strategy 5: making irrelevant comments

Leftists often say the most ludicrous, irrelevant things that lack any common sense whatsoever. If you ask a liberal a pertinent, revealing question, they will often launch into a long recital in an effort to diffuse the question and explain it away. This is a diversion tactic. Here are some actual examples.

Subject: Government funding of abortion
Actors: Kathy (C), Jodi (L)

Kathy: But the government can force others to live by their beliefs [government beliefs] by taking tax dollars and using it to promote their agenda. What's the difference?

Jodi: That is the way it works. Thank and curse the universe. But we are evolving thank goodness.

Analysis: Note the smug tone of Jodi's answer. Her irrelevant reply shows she is not capable of answering Kathy's legitimate question about the government forcing pro-life people to pay for abortions through taxes.

Here is a second example of liberals making irrelevant comments. In this case, the leftist focuses on grammar mistakes in order to disconcert and defeat his conservative opponents.

Subject: Grammar Nazis
Actors: Marcia (C), Ben (L)

Marcia: I can't stand grammar nazis! When they don't have a good answer for something, they always point out grammar mistakes. It's the message that's important!!

Ben: Actually, we point out grammar mistakes because we believe that education and intelligence are important parts of our lives; that proper language facilitates communication, and that learning how to communicate effectively benefits not only yourself but those around you.

Analysis: Ben's answer is arrogant and pompous. He apparently considers himself an expert in the use of language, but he seems to forget that they are on social media, not in a college class on English grammar. His answer reeks of condescension and pretension, and he arrogantly states concepts that are common knowledge. You cannot convince people of anything when you talk down to them, and his answer did not seem to influence any of the people on this thread.

I enjoy running into a grammar Nazi. Why? Because a careful analysis of their writing almost always exposes one or more language mistakes. Every time I have pointed out those errors to them, I am met with deafening silence.

Another example of this is the debate between conservative Candace Owens and Professor Michael Eric Dyson. Both of them are black. Dyson is a race-baiter and an alleged expert on civil rights who believes Trump is emboldening white supremacists. Candace champions the cause of black people, striving to inspire them to throw off the yoke of subservience placed upon them by Democrats.

At one point in the debate, Candace complains that MSNBC has once again pitted her against another black person, thus trying to create division among blacks.

Subject: The independence and freedom of blacks
Actors: Candace Owens (C), Michael Dyson (L)

Candace: Date of tapes (year 2000). People [have the] right to evolve over eighteen years, debating racial division. I'm, I'm being asked to debate another black person.

At this point the learned professor launches into a five-minute, irrational diatribe against President Donald Trump, using as many big words as possible.

Dyson: Well, look. We're dealing with a person [Trump] who has not only radically emboldened the prospects of bigotry, the resurgent, recrudescent hate that he has articulated. If you can't beat 'em con 'em. So he opposes Pat Buchanan on the one hand, and when it's to his own political advantage, and then subsequently, when the real beliefs emerge from Mr. Trump, we see that his vicious animus toward black people, gay people, Mexicans, Muslims, women, and the like, is a kind of cornucopia of hate that has been brashly articulated by a man of manifest lack of serious coherence, chaotic intelligence, and the lack of an ability to really express himself by not only pulling upon the strands of history but refusing to take into consideration what's going on today. So I think in one sense if we're going to be honest about Donald Trump, he has not helped black people. He has not enabled African American people to move forward. He's riding a crest and a wave of economic prosperity put in place by his predecessor Barack Obama. [Candace grins.] He has refused to acknowledge the centrality of police brutality and unarmed black people assaulted by people in this country. So the reality is that Donald Trump, while claiming through rhetoric to be for the blacks, what he has done is [sic] undermined the capacity of African American people to exist in a country where it's not only about the economic effects and the wherewithal that we contend with, it is about the tone, it is about the rhetoric, it is about the atmosphere that has been unleashed here. And Donald Trump has done something very dangerous and destructive. He can't see the difference between an anti-fascist and someone who supports it. He can't see the difference between someone who is against white people and who is for them. So when he draws false equivalencies between both sides, he negates the ability to say, look, I believe in rational, civil discourse in America, but I take a side morally and politically. We are now fifty-three years to date . . . .

Candace: If I may interject for a second . . . .

Dyson: [without a break] Fifty-three years, let me finish, fifty-three years beyond the day [The host tries to intervene.] Let me finish, here we are fifty-three years past the voting rights act. We've seen the resurgence of an attempt to nullify and destroy that black vote. We've seen attempts to somehow circumnavigate around black political citizenry and agency, so all I'm saying is if we're concerned about black people, we've got to be concerned about poverty, equality, lack of access to education, plus the sorts of violence directed to black people in this country.

Host: Candace, go ahead.

Candace: Sorts of violence toward black people? Am I black? I'm curious if I'm black.

Candace goes on to say that twenty-five white Democrats assembled to kick her, a conservative black person, out of a restaurant and threw water and eggs at her because she supports Donald Trump. She spends about a minute refuting the professor, who interrupts her constantly. Then the moderator stops her and says he will give the professor the final word (after the professor had talked for five minutes without interruption). The professor laughingly accuses Candace of "narcissistic preoccupation," and ends by referring to her as "little girl." At that point Candace chides him for using big, meaningless words.[67]

---

67 "You're Just Using Big Words," Candace Owens Smashes Leftist Professor #walkaway, *American Liberty*, Aug. 9, 2018, 10:40, https://www.youtube.com/watch?v=QYgBg8UYys8&t=558s.

It is ironic that Dyson seems to forget that as a black man he managed to become a privileged, big shot professor in "racist America."

Since their Teflon arguments have no substance, liberals often resort to long, incomprehensible explanations in an effort to win the day by the quantity of their verbiage, clearly unaware of the dearth of their reasoning. But Michael Dyson has one miraculous ability: he can read the mind of President Trump.

Strategy 6: denying the validity of your sources

The question of sources can be a tricky one. People tend to rely on sources that confirm their previously held notions. Liberals favor certain sources and are convinced they are getting the truth. The same is true of conservatives. As a result, arguments based only or mostly on sources can be completely futile. Particular sources are only superior if they support their conclusions with factual evidence, but even facts are often rejected by people who hold fanatically to their opinions.

I have heard and evaluated the opinions and evidence of many liberals and conservatives, and I have found that at times conservatives rely on poor assertions, but most often that is a problem with liberals. Liberals tend to discredit all sources they consider to be conservative, to avoid facts and cogent arguments, and instead depend on anger, recriminations, name-calling, mindless talking points, and deflection.

Here are two real examples of liberals denying the worth of conservative sources.

Subject: The electoral college
Actors: Arnold (C), Mike (L)

Arnold: Mike, why are you so focused on Hillary Clinton winning the popular vote? The president has always been elected by the electoral college, not by the popular vote.

Mike: Don't lecture me on the electoral college!! Where do you get your information? From Breitbart?

Arnold: No, from books, documentaries, and essays. I don't even know what Breibart is.

Analysis: Arnold's answer was not bad, but he was defending himself instead of being on the offensive. He probably should have added, "What are your sources?" Liberals will typically not be able to cite sources because they get their information from TV. But if they do give sources, they will usually be from ultraliberal news outlets like the New York Times, CNN, the Washington Post, and Politico. Nevertheless, liberals like to think of their sources as golden.

Subject: GMOs (genetically modified organisms)
Actors: Roberta (C), Kent (L)

Roberta: GMOs are dangerous because it's messing around with nature!

Kent: What are your sources of proof?

[Roberta gives Kent the titles of two books against GMOs.]

Kent: I don't care. GMOs are not dangerous! The books you just cited are not peer-reviewed and thus not scientific.

Analysis: In this case, Roberta could have replied that books are not peer-reviewed; only articles in journals are peer-reviewed. Moreover, such journals and articles are often highly biased. This is because many such journals receive funding from liberal institutions and from a self-interested government. Also, the books against GMOs referenced by Roberta cite hundreds of peer-reviewed articles. Kent had not read any of the books but preferred to dismiss them out of hand.

Strategy 7: talking over opponents

Anyone who completely monopolizes the discussion is being rude and insensitive. This includes people from any place on the political spectrum, including conservatives. They usually do this because they have no good arguments and therefore strive to silence their opponents. They seem to believe that if they allowed their opponents to fully express their views, they might present evidence that the liberals cannot refute.

Since liberals have few valid arguments, they are especially prone to use the talking-over tactic. Piers Morgan, the British analyst, has employed this procedure with nearly every person he debates, and many other "experts" also do this frequently.[68]

In a face-to-face discussion, the conservative debater, when dealing with a real talker, must eventually interrupt and demand some time. He or she might say something like, "It's my turn to talk now." When news pundits rant on in front of President Trump, he raises his hand toward them and says, "Excuse me, excuse me, excuse me, excuse me." Then he continues with his points. Or he just ignores insistent questioners.

Strategy 8: chest-thumping and pretentious threats

This tactic is used often on social media and Amazon reviews. When leftists see books or comments they oppose, they often declare arrogantly that they could easily demolish all the conservatives' assertions: "It would be no problem for me to destroy all those arguments if I wanted to," the liberals say, or something in that vein. But they never do.

On Amazon.com, most of these critics have not purchased or read the book being reviewed, and it is unethical and lazy of them to try discrediting conservative viewpoints without going through the difficult task of researching the topic or reading the book. It is probably a waste of time to respond to such dishonest people.

---

68 "Ben Shapiro and Piers Morgan on guns," *CNN*, Jan. 13, 2013, 4:31, https://www.youtube.com/watch?v=wRyT-45vFzk.

Strategy 9: rehearsing false, biased, or ambiguous evidence

Liberals often recite historical events as evidence that their current claims are right. They do this because they know that the public does not have easy access to that information. And if you take the time and effort to check their facts, you will find they have either lied, misrepresented, cherry-picked, or spun the events in such a way as to support their contentions.

The best way to combat this may be to ask them to give specific references for their sources. Usually, you will find that those sources do not exist or were produced by leftist "scholars" revising history or giving personal, biased interpretations of events.

Strategy 10: ganging up on opponents

This occurs when a conservative finds himself surrounded by several liberals. Often they interrupt him constantly and bury him with one question after another in rapid succession in an effort to confuse and discredit him, or, even better, to rile him. This often happens on The View. Do conservatives use this tactic too? Yes, I have seen them do it, and I did not enjoy it. However, many liberals employ this method as a matter of course.

Strategy 11: stacking the audience

This tactic takes two forms. The first is inserting into political events leftists disguised as conservatives with instructions to scream, rant, disrupt, and even be violent in order to make conservatives look bad.

The second form of this tactic is to select only liberals to fill an audience at a debate sponsored by a leftist host who has a conservative as a guest. When the conservative makes a point, the audience boos, when the host makes a point the audience claps and cheers.

Of course, the liberal mainstream media will always be there to record and broadcast these events.

We saw an example of the second form when conservative Ann

Colter was invited to a debate on the show of liberal Cenk Uygur of the Young Turks. The Young Turks is a progressive left-wing American news and commentary program on YouTube. Nearly every time Cenk makes a comment, the audience goes bonkers, clapping and cheering, but when Ann replies, the audience groans and objects. Note especially the audience's response about eighteen minutes into the following video. So much for an honest, balanced discussion! I often get the impression that some of the audience was paid beforehand to behave in that manner.[69]

Cenk Uygur was even more obnoxious in his debate with Dinesh D'Souza, constantly yelling, interrupting, insulting, and talking over D'Souza.[70]

Strategy 12: stacking the deck or cherry-picking

This occurs when someone selects only the data or evidence that support their conclusions while ignoring those that do not. In other words, it is a conscious suppression of evidence and thus proof of duplicity and lying. We see this when Democrats and other liberals endlessly declare that Trump wanted to ban all Muslim immigration to the US when in reality, he only wanted to put a hold on Muslim immigration coming from seven terrorist nations until they could be properly vetted.[71]

Strategy 13: using insincere indignation

Liberals often use this tactic to shame, humiliate, and silence their opponents. We saw Barack Obama use it against Mitt Romney in

---

69 "Cenk Uygur VS Ann Coulter at Politicon 2015," *The Young Turks,* Oct. 11, 2015, 1:00:11, https://www.youtube.com/watch?v=mm0OkuT8YG8, https://www.youtube.com/watch?v=apj5_XXE8Xc.

70 "Cenk Uygur vs Dinesh D'Souza at Politicon 2016," *The Young Turks*, June 27, 2016, 1:00:11, https://www.youtube.com/watch?v=v4sULDNpvqs.

71 Graham Ledger on the Daily Ledger, "Final Thoughts: Impeachment by the Media," *One America News Network*, Dec. 27, 2019, 2:37, https://www.youtube.com/watch?v=EFjirXt7yPM.

their second debate for the 2012 election. Romney accused Obama of neglecting his presidential responsibilities by his inaction in reference to the Benghazi attack in 2012 that ended in the death of four Americans, including the American Ambassador Chris Stevens, and also Sean Smith, Glen Doherty, and Tyrone Woods.

Instead of admitting his obvious and willful negligence, based on his desire to avoid conflict in view of his upcoming reelection, Obama resorted to an outburst of self-righteous indignation, about one hour and twelve minutes into the debate. Romney tried to press him but was cut off by the moderator. As it turned out, Obama was viewed by most people as a hero and Romney as a bully.[72]

Piers Morgan, formerly of CNN, tried the same tactic of self-righteous indignation in an interview with Ben Shapiro on gun control. But Shapiro did not cower. After the shooting disaster at Sandy Hook Elementary on December 14, 2012, Morgan became prominent in the anti-gun movement. Shortly after the shooting, Morgan invited Shapiro to be a guest on *Piers Morgan Live.* Here is part of this interview:[73]

Subject: Gun control
Actors: Piers Morgan (L), Ben Shapiro (C)

Morgan: Why am I off the rails, Mr. Shapiro?

Shapiro: Honestly, Piers, you've kind of been a bully on this issue because what you tend to do is demonize people who differ from you politically by standing on the graves of the children of Sandy Hook, saying that they don't seem to care enough about the kids. If they cared more about the dead kids, they would agree with you on policy.

---

72 "Raw Video: Second Obama-Romney Presidential Debate," *CNN,* Oct. 17, 2012, 1:37:48, esp. 1:14:55, https://www.youtube.com/watch?v=4BTk2bKJ6uI.

73 Live CNN, "Ben Shapiro and Piers Morgan on guns," *CNN,* Jan. 13, 2013, 4:31, https://www.youtube.com/watch?v=wRyT-45vFzk.

Morgan: How dare you accuse me of standing on the graves of the children that died! How dare you!

Shapiro: I've seen you do it repeatedly, Piers.

Morgan: Like I say, how dare you!

Shapiro: Well, you can keep saying that. But what you do, and I've seen you do it on the program, you keep saying to folks that if they disagree with you politically, this somehow is a violation of what happened in Sandy Hook.

Analysis: The result of this debate was that Morgan looked like a hypocrite and Shapiro like a defender of truth.

Liberal opponents often take on a smug, superior, condescending, pretentious, self-righteous, or even an angry attitude. Many skillful leftist arguers do this on purpose to disconcert their opponents. We should not allow this to throw us. Perhaps we should just smile at their arrogance and continue to cite good arguments backed up by facts. We should always remain calm, polite, and sincere.

In a debate, when liberal opponents resort to hysteria, pronounced anger, hatred, name-calling, all kinds of spurious accusations, crying, whining, or claiming victimhood, you should be happy because you know you have overpowered them with your arguments. You should not rejoice because you won, but because you know that your skills in debate are becoming sharper and thus your influence greater. The goal is first to discover truth, and second to expose liberal falsehoods.

As a frequent alternative, liberals, when they realize they have been beaten, will suddenly become totally mute and say no more. I have often found this to be the case.

Strategy 14: liberals referring to what was said by a conservative celebrity or someone close to their opponent

In an interview with Ben Shapiro, Piers Morgan reads a quote from President Ronald Reagan saying America should ban assault weapons. Shapiro disagrees with that policy. Then Morgan says Shapiro's position is wrong, and Morgan is right to want to ban assault rifles because Reagan agrees with him. Shapiro replies, "Okay, so? I can disagree with Ronald Reagan."[74]

Morgan's leftist logic is faulty because he is not right just because "one of the great right-wing presidents" happened to hold the same position he holds. The same thing happens repeatedly when leftists claim they are right simply because George W. Bush agreed with them.

We find an example of the Left exploiting a relative for political purposes when CNN's Wolf Blitzer interviews Kellyanne Conway, President Trump's advisor. Wolf makes a point of quoting Trump-hating George Conway, Kellyanne's husband, as a ploy to discredit Kellyanne's support of the president. CNN falsely characterizes this as Kellyanne "melting down." The following video is narrated by Brian Tyler Cohen, who clearly reveals his skewed leftist bias.[75]

Kellyanne has every right to be upset at this tricky ambush. Blitzer defends his maneuver by citing how many times in the past he used the same devious tactic on other married couples. Wolf Blitzer's cynical approach is an example of the Left's goal to divide and conquer their opponents.

Strategy 15: pretending ignorance on a subject

In debates, many leftists who have been pontificating on every subject under the sun, will suddenly clam up if a conservative confronts them with a good argument that they know they cannot answer. So they say something like this: "Well, I don't know

---

74 Live CNN, "Ben Shapiro and Piers Morgan on guns," *CNN*, Jan. 13, 2013, 4:31, https://www.youtube.com/watch?v=wRyT-45vFzk.

75 Brian Tyler Cohen, "Kellyanne melts down on air when conversation turns to her husband," Nov. 14, 2019, 7:29, https://www.youtube.com/watch?v=x9fL9tcEUlM.

anything about that" or "Sorry, I haven't researched that topic" or "I prefer not to talk about that." This is obviously using evasion.

Strategy 16: claiming to be more educated than you

Many leftists have spent a year or two in university, or may have even gotten a degree. A degree like, say, music, painting, drama, social justice, human rights, or women's sexuality studies. As a result, they feel they are "educated," and so you should listen and respect what they say about any issue. They do not seem to realize that on these issues they are often parroting what they have heard on TV.

Other liberals try to use their alleged knowledge as a tactic to prove their argument. They may say something like, "You should really inform yourself on these things." This might be true if it is used as the conclusion of an argument, but by itself it does not form an argument at all. What your opponent is really saying is "since you disagree with me, you obviously have not done your homework." It is nothing but pompous pretension and a facile excuse to avoid a real debate.

Strategy 17: exploiting and weaponizing children

Liberals use indoctrinated children as a front for promoting their destructive agenda. Greta Thunberg, a psychologically impaired Swedish seventeen-year-old, was brainwashed into terrifying panic by her parents and other liberals on the topic of global warming. The result was that her handlers put her before the UN so she could declaim angrily against adults opposing the global warming hysteria. As I heard her rant, I felt that her entire speech was a well-rehearsed performance written by adults, an act to impress the world.[76, 77]

---

76 "WATCH: Greta Thunberg's full speech to world leaders at UN Climate Action Summit," *PBS NewsHour*, Sept. 23, 2019, 5:19, https://www.youtube.com/watch?v=KAJsdgTPJpU.

77 Keean Bexte, "Greta Thunberg and her handlers run from questions in Edmonton!" *Rebel News*, Oct. 17, 2019, 9:44, https://www.youtube.com/watch?v=dSH-x6DhfW0.

We saw a similar performance when CCN held a town hall meeting in February 2018 on the assault weapons ban after the Parkland shooting. In this rigged meeting, a group of indoctrinated young people (backed by a loud, rude crowd) fervently and tearfully challenged the position of NRA's Dana Loesch and Senator Marco Rubio. It is clear that CNN exploited those children.[78]

In Sidney, Australia, the teachers and parents of three- to five-year-old children created a petition to the legislature to make a ballot request that the aboriginal flag be flown over the Sidney Harbor Bridge. The teachers claimed that the children recognized the problem themselves and wrote the petition without being coaxed at all. Obviously, these toddlers were exploited to further a political agenda. They could not even read or write.[79]

Many if not most leftists clearly do not care about the psychological well-being and the happiness of the children. Their goals are far more important to them. The primary reason they do this is because they know that conservatives will look bad if they attack or disagree with the ideas expressed by these "honest and innocent" little kids. The Left will stoop to any low, will do absolutely anything, to get their way.

In the following video, we hear the position of conservative Michael Knowles on the global warming hoax and the exploitation of Greta Thunberg, and the emotional reply of flaming liberal Chris Hahn. Hahn angrily attacks Knowles with personal insults and fake righteous indignation at Knowles's supposed attack on an innocent little girl.[80]

---

78 "CNN town hall in wake of Florida school shooting," *CNN*, Feb. 21, 2018, 1:46:50, https://www.youtube.com/watch?v=ZaLh74eXTDo.

79 Andrew Bolt on The Bolt Report, "Adults are listening to 'pint-sized prophets' and 'infant oracles,'" *Sky News Australia*, Oct. 23, 2019, 5:49, https://www.youtube.com/watch?v=jy_tciGHWGM.

80 Contemptor, "Fox News Guest Michael Knowles Calls Greta Thunberg a 'Mentally Ill Swedish Child,'" *Fox News*, Sept. 23, 2019, 5:10, https://www.youtube.com/watch?v=q8sdDGaWqUY.

Not only do the Democrats weaponize children, but they also weaponize apparent crises like the coronavirus pandemic against President Trump.[81]

Strategy 18: arguing by conclusions

This occurs when your liberal opponent gives a generalized characterization of your position. For example, after you make a given point, he may say, "You're just exaggerating" or "That's simply stupid" or "That's totally wrong" or "That's intellectually dishonest." I have had liberals say all these things to me and a lot more. The problem is, your opponent may possess a preconceived conclusion and will never tell you why you are exaggerating or wrong or dishonest. He presents no premise, gives no facts, but is quick to provide a hasty conclusion. In other words, he skips the necessary steps of argumentation and jumps to a conclusion.

Probably the best way to handle this tactic, is to simply ask him why you are exaggerating or why you are wrong. Most likely, you will get no reasonable response.

Strategy 19: claiming to be just kidding

Some liberals, when they are clearly exposed as contradicting themselves or misunderstanding the issue, will declare, "I was just kidding." This is a feeble tactic to save face that makes these liberals look ridiculous. Adam Schiff gave this justification in October of 2019 when he was exposed for making up a fraudulent text for a phone call President Trump made to Zelensky, the Ukranian president, instead of reading the actual text of the phone call. Schiff, taking on the role of a stand-up comedian, called his lying text a "parody."[82]

---

81 Laura Ingraham on The Angle, "Ingraham: The pandemic party," *Fox News*, Feb. 26, 2020, 7:21, https://www.youtube.com/watch?v=Q0k0JK9-8-4.

82 Shannon Bream, "Schiff slammed for 'parody' of Trump call transcript," *Fox News*, Sept. 26, 2019, 5:27, https://www.youtube.com/watch?v=MRh3-1TlUwg.

Strategy 20: asserting that their talking points are constitutional rights

The Left frequently claims that people who support or engage in some dubious or destructive practice have a constitutional right to do so. For example, the proponents of medical leftism claim that children have a constitutional right to receive vaccines in spite of the fact that no such right is expressly stated in the Constitution.

Actually, this is a claim that the Constitution protects "positive rights," in other words, all the rights that people think they deserve. But in reality, the Constitution does no such thing. It protects our freedom from a specific list of federal government incursions, as outlined in the Bill of Rights.

That does not mean that children and their parents do not have the freedom to vaccinate if they choose. In fact, they already exercise that right all the time. So why then does the Left make such a big stink about it? The reason is obvious; it is a case study in group self-projection.

Their claim is actually an effort to discredit and silence anti-vaccine people. Since anti-vaccine people actively oppose the proliferation of vaccines, they are in effect, according to leftists, supposedly denying people of a sacred constitutional right. This is, of course, pure nonsense. Simply because you oppose something, does not mean you are forcing your will upon others.

The people who are actually denying human rights, in this case the freedom to speak and to choose, are the vaccine fanatics because they crusade for vaccine mandates and for the elimination of parental freedom to obtain vaccine exemptions, both of which legally force parents to vaccinate. They also use intimidation and ridicule when they accuse parents of being stupid, ignorant, and uncaring if they resist vaccination. Here is a real-life mini debate.

Subject: Vaccines and constitutional rights
Actors: Rachel (L), Charles (C)

Rachel: I don't agree with antivaxx movement. However, this is a complete violation of our constitutional rights. Just like everything else they do.

Charles: Rachel, how are anti-vaccine people violating your rights?

Rachel: They're telling everybody that vaccines can harm people.

Charles: Are they forcing people to not get vaccinated?

Rachel: In a sense, yes. They're scaring people half to death.

Charles: But are antivaxxers forcing people to avoid vaccines, or are they just teaching them

the dangers of vaccines? Are they getting people thrown in jail?

Rachel: Well, no but their comments are hurting people.

Charles: I see. So you want antivaxxers to shut up.

Rachel: Yes, exactly.

Charles: But doesn't that deprive antivaxxers of their right to free speech? Are you saying you

want to violate their constitutional rights?

Rachel: Of course not. I defend their right to free speech, but they don't have a right to use their free speech to scare people and preach hate. It's very harmful.

Charles: I see. If *you* think their free speech is scary and harmful, then they automatically have no right to such speech.

Analysis: I have already analyzed this pro-vaccine position in my introduction to this debate. I will, however, repeat that Rachel wants Charles to respect the moral rights she is already enjoying as she tries to deprive him of his genuine constitutional right of free speech.

Strategy 21: endlessly repeating the same points in their argument

Since liberals have few valid arguments, they typically repeat the same talking points ad infinitum. They know that repetition brings conviction. This would not work in a debate class, but it is quite effective when done by the media or in private conversations.

In January 2019, President Trump declared that there was a humanitarian crisis at our southern border. Immediately, the hate-Trump media attacked him for manufacturing a crisis that did not exist. The following are some of the Democrat politicians and media outlets repeating ad nauseam almost the same words to decry the president's statement: Nancy Pilosi, Chuck Schumer, Julián Castro, Raúl Grijalva, Adam Schiff, Juan Vargas, James Clyburn; MSNBC, CNN, Morning Joe MSNBC, Joe Lockhart (CNN), Don Lemon (CNN).[83]

All of these people refuse to look at or admit the thousands of tragedies created by some illegal aliens, and they refuse to acknowledge the financial burdens placed on American taxpayers and the crimes and disruption caused by illegals.

During the House and Senate impeachment trials of January 2020, the Democrats repeated the same half dozen irrelevant accusations against President Trump for twenty-four long hours. Meanwhile, the president's approval ratings continued to climb.

Strategy 22: bad-mouthing everything about America and its president

Radical liberals can often be completely irrational when it comes to characterizing America and its president. This is a serious case of tunnel vision. It would be truly comical if it did not have serious implications. To these radicals, America is guilty of every crime imaginable: racism, sexism, xenophobia, Islamophobia, brutality,

---

83 Sean Hannity on Open Monologue, "Hannity: System-wide meltdown at our southern border," *Fox News*, April 2, 2019, 16:02, https://www.youtube.com/watch?v=2Ud_z5DI0D4.

warmongering, genocide, infanticide, persecution and murder of blacks and Hispanics, femicide, and many others.

And they claim the president is even worse. In addition to all the sins just mentioned, he is guilty of past immorality, tyranny, disrespecting the Constitution and the rule of law, dividing the nation, fomenting violence, lying, illegal quid pro quos, sexual assault, corruption, bribery, anti-Semitism, narcissism, being controlled by the Russians, treason, cheating on his taxes, increasing cancer rates, obesity, people blowing their noses too much, teenagers popping their zits in front of people, and so much more.

His most irrational, lying detractors include Michael Cohen, Bill Maher, Michael Moore, Mark Cuban, Robert De Niro, Mitt Romney, Hillary Clinton, the mainstream media, all his political opponents, many brainwashed liberals, and thousands more. The frequency of these idiotic accusations make them extremely boring and entirely vacuous.

Strategy 23: pandering to the public and especially to a voting base

Pandering occurs when someone tries to gain favor or to manipulate people by employing words or actions that provide gratification for the desires of selected targets (the base) and excuses for their weaknesses. We see this in the Democrat debates of 2019, when all the leftist candidates vie with each other to see who can make the most radical, outrageous, and unrealistic promises to their potential supporters.

Strategy 24: fearmongering

This is a consistent and obvious leftist tactic to confuse and manipulate people. The Left treasures fearmongering and crying wolf. They employ the technique when they talk about vaccines, global warming, gun control, immigration, President Trump, Republicans, conservatives, and many other subjects.

On vaccines, they claim millions will die of horrible diseases if they are not vaccinated. On man-made global warming, they assert that all life on earth will perish in twelve years if we don't completely change our lives, overhaul our economy, pay huge carbon taxes, get rid of fossil fuels, stop using cars, airplanes, and so forth.

On gun control, they want more and more useless and ineffective gun control legislation and eventually they hope to prevent people from enjoying their Second Amendment rights. On immigration, they claim we are inhuman if we do not invite the "suffering" world into our country. On President Trump, everything he does or says is the ultimate evil. On Republicans and conservatives, leftists affirm that Republicans are destroying both the Constitution and America. It never seems to stop.

Strategy 25: exploiting the common decency of opponents and mainstream Americans

Most conservatives and other Americans have a strong sense of common decency. This decency is endemic in our population because Western Civilization is based on the principles of Judeo-Christian ethics.

Leftists are fully aware of these facts, and they seek to use our strengths against us in order to further their agenda. Their lapdogs in the media constantly whine about how insensitive and cruel conservatives are when they challenge leftist candidates and leftist goals. Liberals know that the average American would hesitate on social media and elsewhere to openly attack liberals for being selfish, illogical, and fond of promoting or acquiescing to outright violence, for indulging in identity politics, and for the Left's many other destructive practices.

The Left rejoices when they hear nonliberals struggling to be fair or apologize: "Well we must not impugn their motives." On social media, several people, apparently trickle-down liberals, said, "Look! The Squad say they love America, and we should take them at their word. They surely wouldn't lie." Meanwhile the Squad, mostly Muslims, maintain a constant barrage of hateful attacks on America and President Trump, never saying a word about America's historic goodness.

Liberals realize that average Americans prefer civility, compromise, and friendly, non- confrontational exchanges of opinions. By contrast, liberals reject all those principles and exploit the decency of mainstream Americans to further their evil goals. They simply love to fight dirty.[84, 85, 86]

When Donald Trump Jr. appeared on CBS This Morning with Gayle King and two male co-hosts to talk about his new book, *Triggered,* he explained that his father has taught conservatives that it is okay to fight back against leftist attacks. He explained, "We've turned the other cheek for fifty years, and all it's done is to allow us to cede ground."

One of the cohosts, Anthony Mason, jumped in and said, "Everybody in this country agrees the temperature is too high." He added that we are too divided and need healing rhetoric. "What are you doing to heal that divide?" he asked. "It seems like you're doing the opposite."

Trump Jr. explained that it is impossible to heal the divide when the media continually attacks his father.

The cohost pushed his point: "I'm asking you if you are interested in any kind of healing rhetoric that might bring the country closer." Trump Jr. replied that promoting healing is hard when half of Congress accuses Trump of treason, but "We're not going to roll over and die."[87]

So the Left, which has for decades created most of the hatred

---

84 Daughtry and Casselman, *Waking the Sleeping Giant*, pp. 15-16.

85 Herman Cain: "'The Squad' runs the liberal media," *Fox Business Network*, July 16, 2019, 3:43, https://www.youtube.com/watch?v=U-KDErkh48s.

86 Bill Whittle, "Bill Whittle's Hot Mic: Liberals Love to Play Victim," *NRATV*, July 7, 2017, 17:45, https://www.youtube.com/watch?v=FzeRRzBKQwo.

87 "Donald Trump Jr. talks new book, says 'there are very few people' his dad can 'fully trust,'" *CBS This Morning* with host Gayle King, Nov. 6, 2019, 11:13, https://www.youtube.com/watch?v=URN-DYrvLIU.

and division in America, always pleads with Republicans and conservatives to back down, compromise, be nice, and be quiet for the good of the country they pretty much hate. Trump Jr. is right; we must take the battle to them until they wise up, if ever.

Now is the time to stop apologizing, to stop making one-sided compromises, to stop making excuses, and to take the offensive. If we do this, liberals will be shocked and put into a quandary as to what to do. And what will they most likely do? Resort to a great increase of hateful irrationality, name-calling, and violence. This book is an effort to take the battle to them.

Strategy 26: engaging in self-projection

This occurs when one party accuses the second party of the very faults and errors that they themselves have. Unfortunately, this seems to be a universal trait across the entire socialpolitical spectrum, but liberals make a science of it. I believe that conservatives and moderates who do this are inspired by trickle-down liberalism. What follows is based on an actual discussion.

Subject: Name-calling
Actors: Emily (L), Bob (C), Carl (L)

Emily: I think we should never use name-calling. It's rude and uncivilized.

Bob: I agree. At least not in one-on-one discussions.

Carl: They all act like bullies.

Bob: I believe name-calling is valid if it describes groups of people or celebrities who

support evil things. But not in personal conversations.

Emily: No, name-calling should never be used. We have enough division in this world.

Carl: They just get things confused and then go crazy. People sure can be stupid and bigoted.

Bob: Carl, I'm not sure what you're saying. Can you make it clearer?

Carl: You don't get it because you misunderstand me on purpose. You need to try harder.

Bob: I'm just asking you to clarify your ideas.

Carl: Hey, the truth is, you think you know everything. You sure are self-righteous!

Analysis: Here Carl uses name-calling and shows clear signs of arrogance, self-righteousness, and projects his own prejudices and attitudes to Bob.

Strategy 27: reading your mind and impugning your motives

If you disagree with a leftist's conclusions and policies, you must be evil and desire to hurt someone. This is an unfair, dirty tactic of the Left. Juan Williams impugned the motives of conservative Jesse Watters in their discussion of why Democrats insist on having closed-door hearings on the impeachment of President Trump. Two minutes and ten seconds into the video, Williams said to Watters, "You think Bill Taylor is a liar?"[88]

The same video also illustrates how the media functions as one repetitive chorus in attacking Republicans. John Lofgren describes this as "bad intentions" and uses these examples: "You are really just out to make someone look bad, aren't you?" and "You must hate blacks if you oppose the president."[89]

Strategy 28: making prophetic predictions

This is another form of evasion. Instead of addressing the issue, your opponent prophesizes that your current position will someday make you look bad or destroy your life. He might say something like this:

---

88 Greg Gutfeld, "The Five reacts to House GOP storming closed-door impeachment hearing," Oct. 23, 2019, 10:02, https://www.youtube.com/watch?v=qQmajTucXeg.

89 John Lofgren, *Atlas Shouts*, p. 111.

"You'll go to jail for saying that."

"You're going to destroy lives if you continue to preach that."

"This will not go anywhere, so why discuss it?"[90]

Strategy 29: appealing to popularity

In this tactic, leftists might say:

"The president must have colluded with the Russians because everyone in the media says so."

"Most historians I've read agree that the crusaders made unprovoked attacks in Palestine against the Muslims."

In the first example, they are trying to destroy the president. In the second, they want to discredit Christianity. This is the logical fallacy called bandwagon. It assumes something is true (or right or good) because other people agree with it.

Strategy 30: ridiculing the ideas and character of opponents

This is an effort to invalidate and deride your allegations in order to invoke group laughter and thus draw attention away from your reasonable assertions. Here is an example: "The idea that Trump loves America is the silliest, most moronic thing I've ever heard, ha-ha!" Once again, evasion.[91]

Strategy 31: virtue signaling with mind reading

Leftists and their fellow travelers love to tell us how wonderful they are. They express this in many ways. They might say things like:

- "I care about the environment more than most people do."
- "Look, I've been very patient with you."

In my opinion, such statements are not arguments at all.

They are

- weak attempts to prove their arguments are valid.

---

90 John Lofgren, A*tlas Shouts*, p. 111.

91 John Lofgren, A*tlas Shouts*, p. 111.

- efforts at virtue signaling.
- suggestions that you are stubborn and unreasonable.
- underhanded attempts to discredit you and your arguments.
- attempts to shut you up.

I suggest you keep them focused on the topic by saying something like this: "I accept that you are a very patient person, but I don't see how your patience is a valid argument. What is your argument?"

Another form of virtue signaling is a more direct attack: "You are racist and don't care about the poor if you want to build the Wall." Here the attacker pretends to

- prove she is right and glorify her own decency and cultural sensitivity.
- prove her opponent wrong by reading his mind and impugning his motives.
- prove her opponent wrong by using ad hominem insults.
- prove her interlocutor wrong by attacking his decency and humanity.

The following video shows examples of the Left's virtue signaling.[92]

Strategy 32: bullying and intimidation

Liberal bullying and violent threats toward anyone or any group that leftists oppose is becoming increasingly more frequent. We see this at Trump rallies, at speeches given at liberal universities, and elsewhere toward conservative speakers like Ann Colter, Ben Shapiro, Dinesh D'Souza, and Michael Knowles. We see this on many occasions when masked Antifa thugs harass and physically attack people they feel or imagine are conservatives or Trump supporters.

---

92 Will Witt, "White Leftists Act Like Racists," *PragerU*, Jan. 3, 2020, 2:06, https://www.youtube.com/watch?v=nqkF8CmGKwQ.

The online encyclopedia called Conservapedia gives this description of bullying:

> Bullying is the use of force to get one's own way, typically for a selfish purpose at the expense of others. Increasingly liberals try to pass anti-bullying laws as a way of censoring conservative speech and activities, such as quoting from the Bible that criticizes homosexuality or rough physical activities such as football.
>
> Passage and enforcement of anti-bullying laws is a liberal way to increase government control to the point where people, even children, need to constantly worry about whether Big Brother government approves of what they say or do.

Currently, in many venues, especially at universities in the US, the UK, Canada, and other countries, speech that the radical Left disapproves of is called "hate speech," and those who insist on their right to speak freely are hated, demonized, disenfranchised, and physically brutalized by angry activists of the "tolerant" Left. At times they even make death threats. These activists will do absolutely anything necessary to shut down and muzzle their opponents so that "marginalized" people like transgenders can feel coddled and safe.

Sometimes even governments get in on the act, as in Canada, and free speakers can face threats of fines and jail sentences. And if the case is brought to court, liberal judges typically rule against conservatives.[93]

In fact, most countries now have laws against hate speech, but the US is one of a few countries that does not yet ban such speech. However, other entities, such as many universities, Google, YouTube, Facebook, and Twitter, now have irrational rules against what they

---

93 "Free speech under attack," *CBC News: The National* (radio Canada) April 17, 2017, 15:21, https://www.youtube.com/watch?v=k5g9AlCQFaM.

consider unacceptable, controversial speech. In the following video, Dr. Scott Yenor makes the most pertinent comments.[94]

An example of murderous, physical attacks is depicted in Glenn Beck's video on YouTube on November 12, 2018. The title of this video does not begin to represent the leftist violence against Beck's family in a park in New York. Only the presence of four to six security guards saved them.[95]

Bullying also includes reputation destroying. An example of this is seen in a video of Nancy Pelosi discussing "wrap-up smears." The video was produced by ABC, a news outlet airing relentless attacks against Trump. The host on this video claims that the "wrap-up smears" Pelosi is depicting is a Republican tactic, not a Democrat one.

That may be true, but Pelosi's comments are an example of self-projection because smearing opponents is a favorite strategy of Democrats and other liberals, not Republicans. Pelosi gives herself away when she says the Republicans take the smears to the media and "they report it,"[96] but the truth is, the media never reports the Republican opinions that they dislike.

The reputation-destroying tactics of Democrats was on full display in the Brett Kavanaugh hearings for his confirmation as a justice on the Supreme Court. During this hearing, he was falsely accused of sexual attacks when he was a teenager, without a shred of evidence.

Senator Chuck Schumer took threats and intimidation to new heights in a pro-abortion rally on the steps of the Supreme

---

94 Scott Yenor, "Will America Ban Hate Speech?" *The Heritage Foundation,* Oct. 16, 2018, 59:15, https://www.youtube.com/watch?v=vx1BZ1671A0.

95 Glen Beck, "Glenn Beck Responds to Heckler Who Assaulted Tucker Carlson's Daughter," *The Blaze,* Nov. 12, 2018, 5:13, https://www.youtube.com/watch?v=wZwEMo6Eu_E.

96 Host ABC News, Fact or Fiction, "Pelosi admits to using wrap up smear?" *ABC 10 News*, Oct. 10, 2018, :52, https://www.youtube.com/watch?v=WzA-V_1lk40.

Court when he openly menaced Justices Neil Gorsuch and Brett Kavanaugh. He cried out, "I want to tell you, Gorsuch. I want to tell you, Kavanaugh, you have released the whirlwind and you will pay the price."[97, 98]

Strategy 33: race-baiting

Conservapedia defines race-baiting in this way:

> Race baiting [sic] is a term for groundless accusations of racism made by liberals. It is a unique, deliberate and hypocritical focus on race in an attempt to discredit others as "racist." An important component of race baiting is for the indictor to appear "factual," "neutral," "unbiased," a person truly above racism's perversion. Others are unapologetic about racial bias, referring to groups whether guilty or innocent, as rotten people that have to be exposed. It is subtle in its use; race baiting is considered hate speech and affects all races and religious groups, even gender.

Note that this excellent definition shows race-baiting liberals to be purposely engaged in lying, falsely characterizing themselves, and virtue signaling by calling opponents evil ("rotten").

Ben Shapiro writes an entire chapter, Chapter Three, on race bullies. Among many others, he identifies Maxine Waters (p. 90), Spike Lee (p. 93), the *Washington Post* (p. 97), Al Sharpton (p. 113), Barack Obama (p. 113), Jesse Jackson (p. 114), and the *New York Times* (p. 106) as race-baiters.[99]

---

97 Jim Jordan and Mark Meadows. "Jordan, Meadows say Schumer's intimidation tactic won't work," *Fox News*, Mar. 5, 2020, 4:53, https://www.youtube.com/watch?v=CuIFv-sjEhI.

98 Shannon Bream, "Justice Roberts condemns Schumer's comments targeting Gorsuch, Kavanaugh," *Fox News,* Mar. 4, 2020, 2:19 of 4:50, https://www.youtube.com/watch?v=-38Vy0vdGgg.

99 Ben Shapiro, *Bullies*, Chapter Three.

Strategy 34: divide and conquer

This is a deliberate effort to pit race against race, women against men, women against other women, children against parents, schools against parents, politicians against presidential nominees, the poor against the rich, businesses against workers, workers against businesses, the government against the people, straight and gay people against one another, and so forth. The Left wallows in a filthy mire of divisiveness.

To reach their goals, the Left seeks to pass the following legislation in order to apply government force:

- Laws controlling major industries
- Laws for the redistribution of wealth in order to keep all citizens at the same level of mediocrity, all for the nebulous ideas of fairness and equality
- Legislation to constantly raise the minimum wage for all
- Rules for nationalizing all banks, railroads, and industries like steel, auto, and health care
- Laws to increase taxes on the wealthy
- Laws creating a heavy progressive income tax to "level the playing field"
- Legislation that protects the people and provides jobs and health security through extensive entitlement programs
- Laws seeking the pursuit of sexual freedom, resulting in the sexualizing of children, eliminating age of consent rules, and promoting the normalization of pedophilia, all in the pursuit of sexual freedom

Strategy 35: promoting moral relativism

Conservapedia says:

> Relativism is the post-modern idea that there can be no absolutes. 20th century philosophers, and especially liberals, expounded on a theory of moral

> relativism, that there is no absolute right or wrong. Unfortunately, this moral weakening is dangerous, and teaches, in essence, that nothing is wrong, setting mankind ethically adrift.
>
> Liberals try to give relativism credibility by citing the scientific theory of relativity. For example, Harvard Law School Professor Laurence Tribe argued that the theory of relativity justified finding a right to abortion in the U.S. Constitution.

The exploitation of relativist doctrine is nothing but a self-righteous, bully tactic. The very fact that leftists claim moral relativism to be an absolute truth contradicts their belief that there is no absolute truth.

Group moral relativism is another form of relativism. For example, some proponents of Democratic Socialism falsely claim that there are many schools or subgroups in their political movement. That idea is used to justify socialist ideology on any issue.

For example, if some conservative were to challenge the wisdom of open borders, the defender of Democratic Socialism can simply assert that only some segments of their movement believe in open borders, not all segments, and those subgroups do not stand for all Democratic Socialists. Thus, looked at as a whole, Democratic Socialism should still be considered a wise and viable option on the political scene.

But the truth is, all the alleged schools of Democratic Socialism follow exactly the same road. In addition, many Communists and hard-core socialists like Bernie Sanders now claim to be Democratic Socialists.

You can witness a rather verbose defense of group relativism by Dr. Cornel West, a Democratic Socialist, on Tucker Carlson.[100]

---

100 Tucker Carlson, "Tucker takes on Cornel West over Democratic Socialism," *Fox News*, July 6, 2018, 9:44, (https://www.youtube.com/watch?v=kuc6C2_Txmw.

Now for a realistic verbal exchange illustrating moral relativism:

Subject: Illegal Hispanic immigration
Actors: Amy (L), Logan (C)

Amy: These poor people are human beings too, just looking for happiness. And yet they are met with violence by our government. Many are shot or put in jail. They lack the basic necessities of life and should be allowed to enter our country freely if we care about people.

Logan: I'm not so sure they're all that destitute. In the picture you showed on Facebook, many of them have new sneakers and coats, cell phones, and lots of other stuff. They also look pretty chubby and well-fed. The truth is they just seem to want American welfare and American jobs.

Amy: Well, I don't seek truth anymore. I just seek beauty and love.

Logan: You don't seek truth? Is that an admission that your first comments about immigrants are not true?

Analysis: If you do not seek truth, you will not find truth, and thus your opinions will depend only on your personal feelings and perceptions. In that event, two people having contradictory views on a given subject can both be right. That is moral relativism.

Strategy 36: the duplicitous use of statistics and polls

Leftists love to quote statistics as if they were absolute proof of their contentions. In the Sanpete Messenger of October, 2019, the chairwoman of the Sanpete County Democrats declared that 88% of all Utahns support universal background checks for the purchase of all guns, and 80% of strong Republicans also support the same thing. As proof, she cites a political information group called Utah Policy, but when you check that source you see that the poll mentioned asks if Utahns support "background checks for all gun sales," not *universal* background checks.

Therefore, her two statistics are meaningless.[101]

We already have criminal background checks across the country in NICS (National Instant Criminal Background Check System). But NICS is not a universal background check system. In other words, she conflates a proposed system with one already in place. She also asserts that data shows that background checks do reduce gun violence if strictly enforced. The problem is, she neglects to document the alleged data.

In his book *How The Left Was Won,* Richard Mgrdechian states:

> As we have seen, liberals love to quote statistics. Unfortunately, as we have also seen, the statistics they tend to use are either wrong, irrelevant, skewed by some inaccurate measurements or intentionally biased in order to help justify their position on any given issue.
>
> Still, there is no doubt that liberals will continue to inundate us with these sorts of meaningless numbers in order get whatever it is they want, and one of the most subtle techniques for doing this is through the use of polls.

As an example, Mgrdechian cites one of the polls liberals loved to reference to justify their hatred of George W. Bush. The 2006 Gallup Poll, from February 9 to February 12, asked, "Do you approve or disapprove of the way George W. Bush is handling his job of president?" The response was 39% approved, 56% disapproved, and 4% had no opinion. Obviously these numbers are not great, but this poll was done in a vacuum, not attempting to

---

101 Utah Policy, https://utahpolicy.com/index.php/features/today-at-utah-policy/21607-most-utah-voters-believe-some-new-gun-control-measures-won-t-violate-the-2nd-amendment.

take up possible background context and other potential causes. It only reported the results.

Another Gallup Poll done around the same time found that only just 27% of Americans approved of the way Congress was performing. So, Mgrdechian concludes, "By comparison, Bush looks like a genius."[102]

We must be leery when leftists claim that statistics are proof of anything. Some statistics are inaccurate or wrong because the study was not done properly. The liberal purveyors of statistics do not tell us who performed the study, what were its parameters, and how large the sampling was. We're just supposed to believe the numbers because they publish them.

You can witness five minutes of lies based on numbers in this video on the positions of seven Democrat candidates for the presidency:[103]

In the debate on Politicon between Tucker Carlson of Fox News and Cenk Uygur of the Young Turks, Cenk quotes many statistics to prove his points on immigration. But he fails to cite sources for these statistics, and most of them are questionable. Besides statistics, this debate illustrates the Left's use of virtue signaling and stacking the audience.[104]

Strategy 37: deflecting from the subject

In this tactic of evasion your opponent bypasses the issue you have presented and introduces a completely different subject—either purposely or ignorantly—which is offered as an apparent refutation of your point. The reference below concerns the Greta Thunberg team's refusal to answer questions as to why they are

102 Richard Mgrdechian, *How The Left Was Won,* pp. 115-116.

103 LibertyPen, "Top 10 Lies from the Democratic Party Presidential Debate," *MSNBC,* Nov. 25, 2019, 4:30, https://www.youtube.com/watch?v=vbXWDj1QbkE.

104 "Cenk Uygur vs Tucker Carlson at Politicon 2018," *The Young Turks,* Oct. 22, 2018, 59:34, https://www.youtube.com/watch?v=7ZxhLli-7CY.

staging a protest campaign in Calgary just before a federal election in oil-producing Alberta province, Canada.[105]

Here is another mini debate showing leftist deflection:

Subject: Transgenderism
Actors: Milly (L), Alfred (C)

Alfred: Transgenderism is an emotional sickness.

Milly: What makes you say that?

Alfred: Biology proves there are only two genders, male and female. Just because someone emotionally "identifies" as another gender does not make it true. Can a transgender female (really a male) give birth to a child? Nope. Never has happened.

Milly: What about people who are born with a penis and a vagina and can actually give birth?

Alfred: You're talking about biological sexual abnormalities. That has nothing to do with transgenderism. Transgenderism deals with emotional problems, not physical ones.

Analysis: Milly has changed the subject from transgenderism to the subject of people born with sexual deformities. Transgender people do not have sexual deformities. Alfred then exposes her deflection from the issue at hand.

Strategy 38: perverting good principles

This occurs when someone pushes a good principle to extremes and gets the opposite results from what was intended. The Left are experts at doing this. There are two general categories here: principles of a more physical nature that involve one person or many people, and principles of a moral or intellectual nature that have an impact on most people.

---

105 Keean Bexte, "Greta Thunberg and her handlers run from questions in Edmonton!" *Rebel News*, Oct. 17, 2019, 9:43, https://www.youtube.com/watch?v=dSH-x6DhfW0.

The first category is obvious and not my concern in this book: exercise too much and you'll injure yourself, eat too much and you'll become obese, etc.

I am more concerned with moral and spiritual principles like tolerance, freedom, equality, and diversity. Tolerance pushed too far can become intolerance as when someone shows tolerance toward sexual perversion. Freedom pushed too far becomes license or anarchy.

Freedom of speech is a good thing. But when that speech disagrees with leftist policies, liberals purposely pervert the idea of free speech and call it "hate speech." Complete equality in every way, especially equality of outcome, is impossible and leads to government control and manipulation. Diversity pushed too far can be destructive of national identity, personal freedom, and safety if it involves, for example, allowing illegals from inferior cultures with destructive values to swarm our nation.[106, 107]

Strategy 39: guilt by association

Liberals use this devious strategy to embarrass and discredit their opponents. If a conservative has any connection, no matter how tenuous, with someone characterized as a "crazy radical," then that conservative must also be a crazy radical. Here are some examples of this tactic:

- Liberals displaying a photo of a conservative standing next to someone with a dubious reputation, such as showing George W. Bush laughing with liberal John Kerry.
- On social media, a commenter juxtaposes conservatives with known leftists as if they were of the same ilk. For example, in a discussion on Phil Valentine's objections to legalizing

---

106 Jordan Peterson, "The fatal flaw in leftist American politics," *BigThink,* April 12, 2018, 9:44, https://www.youtube.com/watch?v=8UVUnUnWfHI.

107 Jordan Peterson, "Dangerous People Are Teaching Your Kids," *PragerU,* June 11, 2018, 5:02, https://www.youtube.com/watch?v=LquIQisaZFU.

drugs in his book *The Conservative's Handbook*, the commenter says, "I suggest you read what Dr. Ron Paul has to say on the subject. Phil Valentine is in the business of political entertainment, much like Glen Beck, Rush Limbaugh, and Rachel Maddow. Dr. Paul has a very different view that comes from a libertarian ideal and the knowledge that comes from a lifetime as a doctor."

Analysis: So conservatives Valentine, Beck, and Limbaugh are juxtaposed with flaming liberal Rachel Maddow and are thus discredited.

- On the View, Joy Behar tries to discredit Democrat candidate Tulsi Gabbard because Tulsi seems to appear only on the show of Tucker Carlson, who is a "liar and a propagandist." And then Behar continues her attack by noting that Richard Spencer, the white nationalist leader, "says he could vote for you."[108, 109]
- In a Quick Quotes article, *The New American* quotes Joe Biden as saying: "The president and his—the Ku Klux Klan and the rest of them—they think they've beaten us again. But they have no idea. We're just coming back." But this is hardly one of Biden's many gaffes. The article explains:

  > While speaking to a large congregation of black Americans at a Baptist church in South Carolina, Joe Biden employed the reprehensible tactic of mentioning the president and the KKK in the same sentence. He knows that listeners will remember the negative association, not the fact that Biden didn't actually accuse the president

108 Daniel Luepker, "Tulsi Gabbard Destroys Joy Behar," *Hard Lens Media*, Nov. 7, 2019, 7:47, https://www.youtube.com/watch?v=MUTChYKCTeo.

109 Lauren Southern, "Literally Everything is White Supremacy," *Rebel News*, Sept. 22, 2016, 4:40, https://www.youtube.com/watch?v=TiuWKiq2d8o.

> outwardly of having anything to do with the Klan.[110]

Strategy 40: flip-flopping

On sociopolitical issues, there is a difference between flip-flopping versus evolving. Flip-flopping is a sudden reversal of position while evolving is a progressive change over a period of time. The first suggests lying and ambition. The second suggests (hopefully) positive growth. Both Republican and Democrat politicians are guilty of flip-flopping.

Which camp does the most flip-flopping? We can only find out by doing a great deal of comparative research, but nearly every politician has been accused of flip-flopping by their opponents. In my biased opinion, lefties engage in flip-flopping more frequently than conservatives.

One of the most notorious and hypocritical flip-floppers is Mitt Romney, a Republican in name only.

Strategy 41: depending on necromancy

Webster's defines necromancy as the conjuration of the spirits of the dead for purposes of magically revealing the future or influencing the course of events.

This is the perfect word for describing the Democrats' tactic of hypocritically citing the Founding Fathers and the Constitution to support their socialist agenda. It is especially ironic because the Democrats are the crowd that constantly belittles and undermines the Founders, the Constitution, and American traditions.

Necromancy raised its ugly head during the December 2019 hearing of the House Judiciary Committee on Capitol Hill. The Democrats enlisted the aid of three anti-Trump law professors to claim that Trump's connection with Ukrainian leaders constituted grounds for impeachment. These legal "experts"

---

110 The *New American*, Feb. 17, 2020, p. 9.

constantly supported their contentions by citing the judgments of our Founding Fathers.

The fourth witness, Professor Jonathan Turley, was called by the GOP. He accused the other three witnesses, Pamela Karlan, Michael Gerhardt, and Noah Feldman, of engaging in necromancy.[111, 112]

Strategy 42: relying on religious beliefs

This strategy is related to necromancy. Nancy Pelosi declares that as a Catholic mother she defends women's right to choose. Choose what? To murder their babies in the womb. She seems oblivious to the fact that the Catholic Church is against abortion.[113]

Alexandria Ocasio-Cortez declared before Congress that if Jesus were to return and see what was going on in our society, he would be rejected and maligned. However, in view of the policies she promotes, the sincerity of her Christian beliefs is seriously in question.[114]

Strategy 43: creating a cancel culture

People who promote the concept of cancel culture see themselves as truly "woke." Thus, these woke liberals have taken upon themselves the noble role of arbiters of what is right and what is wrong, what is acceptable and what is not acceptable. As a result, they attempt to cancel, demonize, or wipe out any group, person, or idea they oppose. In this effort, cancelers promote demonstrations, protests, violence, mobbing, digging up past dirt or the ancient usage of "forbidden" words, gossip, discrediting, and boycotting

---

111 Laura Ingraham, "The Angle: You know it's over when . . ." *Fox News*, Dec. 4, 2019, 7:10, https://www.youtube.com/watch?v=fOL_BF2jN58.

112 "Speaker of the House Nancy Pelosi's final floor speech for the health care reform bill," *PBS NewsHour*, Mar. 21, 2010, 2:53, https://www.youtube.com/watch?v=rZt8QdD39Mc.

113 Nancy Pelosi, "Women in the world 2012: Nancy Pelosi on Catholics and Contraception," *The Daily Beast*, March 9, 2012, 2:00, https://www.youtube.com/watch?v=TqYB0mdDR2w.

114 Pat Gray, "AOC gives us a lesson on Jesus," *BlazeTV*, March 2, 2020, 4:33, esp. :22, https://www.youtube.com/watch?v=hWztGWPRQ9s.

in order to silence all opposing viewpoints and to destroy the civil rights of others.

We saw this mentality—which is based purely on emotion and fake outrage—in the Brett Kavanaugh hearings when liberals tried to prevent his selection as a justice of the Supreme Court by harping on his alleged sexual misconduct that supposedly happened decades earlier.[115]

Strategy 44: guilt by omission

In this strategy, the Left claims that since the media did not report on alleged criminal behavior, that behavior does not exist.[116]

Strategy 45: self-projection

This is to project or attribute your personal weaknesses, ideas, and sins onto others. Liberals are experts at doing it against conservatives.[117]

Strategy 46: playing the victim

Whenever liberals find themselves backed into an embarrassing corner and lacking a credible argument, they typically begin to cry and whine, accusing you of being an evil bully who uses insults and name-calling. Ironically, to this tactic they often add an abundance of insults and vitriol against you.[118]

Conservatives sometimes do this too, but it is more often a tactic among liberals. Their goals are obvious: to justify themselves

---

115 Brigitte Gabriel, "Cancel Culture is Out of Control!" *Act for America*, Dec. 10, 2019, 3:20, https://www.youtube.com/watch?v=aKT2NhwEovs.

116 Graham Ledger on The Daily Ledger, "National Security Expert, Charles Faddis, on the Inspector General's Report," *One America News Network*, Dec. 16, 2019, 5:29, https://www.youtube.com/watch?v=2OYvRWSk98U.

117 Tucker Carlson, "Tucker: No one is above the law except Democrats," *Fox News*, Dec. 10, 2019, 11:25, esp. 5:20-6:50, https://www.youtube.com/watch?v=vwg5ub_xGdU.

118 Bill Whittle, "Bill Whittle's Hot Mic: Liberals Love to Play Victim," *NRATV*, July 7, 2017, 17:45, https://www.youtube.com/watch?v=FzeRRzBKQwo.

and to silence, manipulate, and discredit you. I respond by telling them that I am criticizing their ideas, not impugning or maligning their character.

Strategy 47: controlling the narrative

The Left insists on controlling the narrative and even the language used. In their rules, you can only address certain preferred subjects, but not others. For example, the Left feels it is good and noble to defend the rights of the LGBTQ community, but they angrily forbid anyone from attacking Muslims, in spite of the fact that Muslim countries slaughter gays. Many leftists even take offense at conservatives calling them "liberals."[119, 120]

Strategy 48: inventing meaningless slogans

Nearly every day, liberals and their fellow travelers come up with nutty, irrelevant, and meaningless catchphrases that they hope will gain popularity. Apparently, they think they are pronouncing words of deep wisdom that will verify whatever point they conjure up. In the preceding chapter, I have listed many of their nonsensical slogans and memes.

Strategy 49: ignoring their own inconsistencies and contradictions

Most radical liberals are basically hypocrites. They make boastful, pompous claims that are proven false by their actual behavior. Here is a list of some of their frequent contradictions:

- Liberals claim to care about the poor but give much less to charity than conservatives. However, they are very charitable when using other people's money.

---

119 Foluke Tuakli, "Leftists Want To Control Everything You Say," *TheDC Shorts*, Sept. 12, 2019, 3:11, https://www.youtube.com/watch?v=T78_XkZCvRw.

120 Andrew Klavan, "Politics Is about Controlling the Narrative," *Daily Wire*, June 29, 2018, 3:11, https://www.youtube.com/watch?v=_fZMarljMaE.

- They claim that anyone who disagrees with them is racist but they exploit blacks, Hispanics, and Jews for their votes.
- They say whites oppress blacks but deny the fact that whites were the first ethnic group to rid the world of slavery.
- They declare that global warming will soon destroy all life on earth while they personally consume vast amounts of energy from fossil fuels and support projects like the Green New Deal that will cause worldwide chaos, societal disruption, and economic bankruptcy.
- Many of them (and especially socialists and Commies at the UN) declare we will all die of starvation if we do not reduce world population, but they never offer themselves to submit to sterilization and euthanasia.
- Many of them, especially leftist feminists, declare that white men oppress women while they turn a blind eye to the millions of females murdered through abortion and the slavery and oppression of all women in Muslim countries.
- They strive to pass endless gun control legislation but refuse to admit that thousands of law-abiding people are saved by guns, that such laws deprive Americans of their Second Amendment rights, leaving them defenseless, and that criminals never obey those laws. They also refuse to get rid of the guards who protect them with guns.
- They claim to favor better education while they adopt Common Core that undermines good education, and they support funding universities where liberal professors poison the minds of immature students with socialist ideology.
- They claim to champion free speech while they do everything possible to silence any speech they disagree with, and they typically encourage outright intimidation and violence to get their way.
- They crusade for the alleged rights of the LGBTQ people while they sneer at the First Amendment rights of Christians to practice their religion.

- They solemnly claim to honor and defend the Constitution while at every turn they strive to undermine and discredit that document by doing destructive things like asking for the elimination of the electoral college.
- They pride themselves on loving America while they undermine our institutions and exalt inferior cultures as being picturesque and "morally equivalent."
- They vaunt fair elections while they promote the stuffing of ballot boxes, encourage illegal immigration to give themselves new voting blocks, and resist voter ID laws.
- They claim to champion the "rights" of minorities but exploit them for their votes.
- They say it is bad to criticize or insult liberals but it is okay to do that to conservatives and patriots.
- They give lip service to American independence while they push for globalism which would destroy our independence and our individualism.
- They insist that the Bible is fiction but the Koran is gospel truth.
- They proscribe any show of Christian faith but exalt Islamic symbols and practices.
- They glorify themselves by claiming to love everyone, including Muslims, but everything they do shows they hate Christians.
- They have the habit of decrying all Christian citations but use them when convenient (for example, Nancy Pelosi exploiting her Catholic faith).
- They insist that the mainstream media is completely fair, objective, and unbiased but the alternative media is a hotbed of hatred and misinformation.
- They claim to worship science but deny the real science relating to global warming while embracing junk climate science.
- They crusade to vaccinate every person on earth but refuse to acknowledge the millions of people (especially children) who are killed or damaged by vaccines.

- They condemn lying but indulge in it constantly.
- They love to call conservative ideas "conspiracy theories" while they make up and profit politically from their own endless conspiracy theories.
- They glorify tolerance and diversity while they condemn Israel and Jews.
- They adore socialism but can't even define it or say where it has succeeded.
- They claim to promote equal rights but tend to place the "rights" of illegals over those of Americans.
- They say they believe that there are no absolute truths but claim their views to be absolute truth.
- They claim to hate fascism but applaud fascist tactics and never criticize the violence of Antifa.
- They seek a socialist Utopia while they promote policies that, if successful, would turn Western Civilization into a dystopia.[121]

A special letter to the editor showing the fruits of the Left:

Posted on January 19, 2011 by Questioning With Boldness:

"The following is a transcript of a letter to the editor that first appeared on June 9, 2010, in the Iosco County News Herald. It is attributed to someone by the name of Ken Huber from Tawas City, Michigan. I [the editor of Questioning with Boldness] feel that is equally relevant 6 months later and maybe it can be a barometer for how the Republican Congress is doing at making inroads into changing the current state of ship in the U.S."

> Editor,
>
> Has America become the land of special interest
> and home of the double standard?
>
> Lets see: if we lie to the Congress, it's a felony and if

121 Ted Cruz, "Ted Cruz DESTROYS Far-Left's Dream of a Socialist 'Utopia'," *BlazeTV*, Dec. 27, 2019, 3:11, https://www.youtube.com/watch?v=XwK-sHbsbYI.

the Congress lies to us its just politics; if we dislike a black person, we're racist and if a black person dislikes whites, its their 1st Amendment right; the government spends millions to rehabilitate criminals and they do almost nothing for the victims; in public schools you can teach that homosexuality is OK, but you better not use the word God in the process; you can kill an unborn child, but it is wrong to execute a mass murderer; we don't burn books in America, we now rewrite them; we got rid of communist and socialist threats by renaming them progressive; we are unable to close our border with Mexico, but have no problem protecting the 38th parallel in Korea; if you protest against President Obama's policies you're a terrorist, but if you burned an American flag or George Bush in effigy it was your 1st Amendment right.

You can have pornography on TV or the internet, but you better not put a nativity scene in a public park during Christmas; we have eliminated all criminals in America, they are now called sick people; we can use a human fetus for medical research, but it is wrong to use an animal.

We take money from those who work hard for it and give it to those who don't want to work; we all support the Constitution, but only when it supports our political ideology; we still have freedom of speech, but only if we are being politically correct; parenting has been replaced with Ritalin and video games; the land of opportunity is now the land of hand outs; the similarity between Hurricane Katrina and the gulf oil spill is that neither president did anything to help.

And how do we handle a major crisis today? The

> government appoints a committee to determine who's at fault, then threatens them, passes a law, raises our taxes; tells us the problem is solved so they can get back to their reelection campaign. What has happened to the land of the free and home of the brave?

Strategy 50: claiming that the injunctions of Christianity suppress free speech

This tactic is another effort to discredit the Bible and Christianity, whose doctrines are the moral foundation of Western Civilization.

It starts by citing the Old Testament and declares that the Ten Commandments gave Israel rules that they must obey or receive dire punishment—an eye for an eye. And therefore, all those rules supposedly suppressed free speech. The same is true of the commandments given by Jesus in the New Testament. The wild claim continues by saying that it is only through a rebellion against the Judeo-Christian tradition that free speech was assured, not by adherence to those traditions because all those commandments condemn free expression.

This analysis is not hard to refute. The Ten Commandments did not suppress free speech; they restrained destructive overt behavior. It is true that the ninth commandment, "Thou shalt not covet," deals with what takes place in a man's heart, but it is a teaching meant to be embraced in order to prevent the possibility of future adultery or thievery. It is not a form of brainwashing or compulsion because each man still has the freedom to choose. A teaching is a guide not a compulsion. If God wanted to control how men think and speak, he could have deprived them of free will and forced them not to covet.

The Israelites had just been freed from 400 years of slavery in Egypt and they were totally lacking in political organization and in the ability to govern themselves. All they had was Moses. So the Lord, through Moses, gave them these initial rules to help them control negative behavior, not free speech.

Christ's admonitions were the same. He taught men how to live and have faith. He did not force them to do so.[122]

Strategy 51: firing multiple questions in a row without waiting for responses

Some liberals habitually use this tactic, trying to overwhelm their opponents with a barrage of questions while not listening to the answers. Liberal Alan Colmes and Fox contributor Juan Williams are experts at rapidly asking one question after another with their ears completely closed.[123]

Strategy 52: exploiting the "cult of celebrity"

Suzanne Dean, publisher of the Sanpete Messenger, railed against candidate Donald Trump in her Publisher's Opinion piece in March, 2016. Basing her ideas on CNN, she reviewed a litany of accusations against Trump. She also condemned Trump supporters as being mesmerized by Trump's celebrity: "What dumbfounds me is how Trump is gathering such a huge national following." Then she cited liberal Carl Bernstein of "Watergate fame" who depicted Trump supporters as being motivated by fascist tendencies and being dazzled by celebrity. She also claimed to receive support from Governor Mike Leavitt and some unnamed expert professor.

Unfortunately, Suzanne Dean seemed oblivious to the fact that she supported her article by referring to three celebrities.

---

122 Candace Owens and Charlie Kirk, "Ocasio-Cortez Supporter CONFRONTS Candace Owens, Watch How She Responds," *Vender*, Dec. 10, 2019, 25:05, https://www.youtube.com/watch?v=8oCzGTsOm9U (Note: due to liberal censorship, this video has been since removed from YouTube.).

123 The Five, "Jesse Watters, Juan Williams clash over Trump foreign intel remark," *Fox News*, June 13, 2019, 8:33, https://www.youtube.com/watch?v=YJu6rLGJSd8.

Strategy 53: duplicitous evading of uncomfortable questions

A hilarious example of this tactic is seen in Tucker Carlson's interview with Newsweek writer Kurt Eichenwald. Eichenwald refuses to answer a simple question, changes the subject, diverts to a personal attack on Carlson, and shows himself to be a fake journalist who repeats lies.[124, 125]

Strategy 54: denying the clear, explicit language of violent threats

When Iran for decades screamed "death to America" and "death to Israel," liberals asserted that Iran did not really mean "death," but was only expressing exasperation with American meddling in Iranian affairs. This of course flies in the face of the fact that Iran is the world's premier terrorist nation and has already killed hundreds of Americans and thousands of others.

In the following interview with Iranian president Hassan Rouhani, a CBS host asks Rouhani whether or not the death threat is meant literally. Rouhani, good trickster that he is, says the slogan is not against the American people, and that the Iranian people respect the American people, but the policies of the United States have been against the national interests of the Iranians.

This statement is full of double-talk because Rouhani conflates the Iranian people with the tyrannical Iranian regime that suppresses the people. American policies have never targeted the Iranian people but only the regime.

Of course, the liberal CBS host, in his milquetoast interview, does not challenge any of Rouhani's statements.[126]

---

124 Tucker Carlson, "Tucker Carlson confronts Newsweek bias," *Fox News,* Dec. 15, 2016, 8:33, https://www.youtube.com/watch?v=7Ophbx1iaF8.

125 Jesse Watters, "Watters' Words: The fake news awards: Jan. 6, 2018. It is my honor to nominate Newsweek writer Kurt Eichenwald for President Trump's [fake news award]." *Fox News,* Dec. 15, 2016, 6:07, https://www.youtube.com/watch?v=iz4mEyrNH90.

126 Andrew Wilkow, "OK, Leftists, Name a Better Nation. We'll Wait," *BlazeTV,*

Strategy 55: using tricky euphemisms

We have already seen this tactic while discussing deceptive liberal slogans, but this subterfuge is ubiquitous and hidden in nearly all leftist claims. For example, to express the need to reduce global warming by reducing the population, eco-social strategist Stuart Scott explained that liberal activists must "educate females," meaning "indoctrinate them," and teach people to engage in tax-funded "family planning," meaning "abortion and contraception."[127]

Jan. 25, 2020, 7:08, https://www.youtube.com/watch?v=pNdD5GtnYNQ.

127 Alex Newman, "Faith, Family and Freedom Under Warmist Assault," *The New American*, Feb. 3, 2020, pp. 20-21.

CHAPTER FIVE

Engaging Leftists (Rules for Debate)

ACTUALLY, RATHER THAN RULES, WHAT follows are suggestions based on my experiences and the experiences of other conservatives. In my previous review of liberal slogans and strategies, I provide many responses to leftist arguments, but here I will expand those responses.

It is important that I remind you again that it is impossible to convince hard core liberals of anything or change their minds. It seems that no power on earth can get them to change. No matter what the subject.

There are also liberals, not necessarily hard core, who are so fanatical and brainwashed, it may be best not to engage them in the first place. These are the ones who scream, rant, use insults, cry, make threats of violence, and never even try to listen. As Benjamin Franklin said, "You cannot reason a man out of a position he has not reasoned himself into."

Do not be concerned. These are our objectives:

- To promote and defend freedom. All the other goals depend upon this prime purpose.

- To seek and defend the truth.
- To defend America and its heritage.
- To inform and perhaps sway anyone monitoring the debate, people who have not yet made up their minds. Often there are many of these undecided individuals listening carefully but remaining silent.
- It should never be our goal to win an argument or impress other people with our skills, knowledge, and intelligence. By being willing to debate, and sometimes getting a ton of flack for our efforts, we will also gain insight into the typical progressive tactics while we sharpen our own abilities.

Now for the list of rules.

Rule 1: Analyze your own motives, goals, and attitudes.

Before we engage in debate, we should accept our own fallibility. Always hold in mind that your views, opinions, information, and even your "facts" might possibly be wrong. Do not be inflexibly certain you are always right. Many people have found themselves in the humiliating position of fervently maintaining a position they really believed was right, only to discover later that they were completely wrong. This is not to say you should be wishy-washy. You must "stick to your guns" if you truly believe you are in the right. Just make sure you have valid, verifiable facts to back up a disciplined argument.

Experience shows us that the person who presents his opinions noisily, vigorously, insistently, and adamantly, or who tries to talk over an opponent, or repeats the same point over and over again is usually dead wrong. He argues that way because he has no facts to back him up. He may receive glory and praise from his friends, but honest people will secretly or openly consider him to be a bombastic chucklehead and reject his views out of hand.

Some leftists are willfully evil, but it is not always easy to spot them. Therefore, we should assume our opponent is basically a "good person" who is simply mistaken and probably doesn't realize the error of his ways, until he proves himself otherwise. We should remember that good people can do bad things without realizing it. In other words, decent people, depending on their background and the quality of their information, can make serious mistakes. I realize you already know this, but I am just stating a reminder.

Then, when you decide to enter into a debate, you should determine beforehand to always remain calm, rational, and considerate when you respond to your opponents or ask questions, no matter how unfair they behave. Do not act in such a way that they can ever have good reason to call you "rude." Never exchange barbs with them. Speak and write deliberately and clearly. Avoid hyperbole and purposeful incitement. Abstain from trying to impress people with fancy, learned words. If your opponent gives you nonsense, keep after him patiently but don't run it into the ground. Your audience or readers will soon see his duplicity.

Some liberals and the evil things they do will make you angry, but it is vital that we avoid displays of hatred or express feelings of anger toward them. Some conservatives engage in this all too often. But to indulge in this seriously undermines the cause of liberty and will give the opposition fuel to attack conservatives as being irrational thugs, and most reasonable people who witness such behavior will be turned off.

Here are some real-life examples from YouTube and social media of the counterproductive practice of attacking individuals rather than their arguments:

- Hey Dinero [De Niro]! Is that your IQ or your number of legitimate children?
- Nancy [Pelosi] and Maxine [Waters] have had so many facelifts forehead is stapled to their Butt Dianne [Feinstein] is just crypt keeper scary yikes.
- Pencil neck geek and Insane Lady [Pelosi].
- I'd really like to kick liddle Adam Schitt [Schiff] in his windpipe.

- Is it just me, or does everyone want to see this little Schitt [Schiff] dead!?
- Bastards are the REAL enemy of the people.
- [Rashida] Tlaib needs an intervention between her neck and her cerebellum.
- He's [a CEO] full of shit. What a jackass!
- [Bernie Sanders] Commie Asshole. Firing Squad.

I like the advice Lincoln gives in his Second Inaugural Address (1865): "With malice toward none, with charity for all, with firmness in the right as God gives us to see the right, let us strive on to finish the work we are in, to bind up the nation's wounds." As applied to debating, this means that we should be kind but still pursue our objectives with great firmness.

Rule 2: Identify your opponent.

Is your opponent a hard core liberal, an uninformed liberal, a misinformed liberal, or something in between? Is he a friend or a relative? Is he a conservative, a socialist, a Communist, a Libertarian, a Democrat, or a Republican? It is important to ascertain these things because you need to gear your responses to the views and biases of your disputant.

You can usually identify your interlocutor's degree of leftism by his first few comments. If he is a hard core leftist, he will typically be close-minded, make irrelevant remarks, and become angry, hostile, and aggressive very quickly, depending largely on hyperemotion rather than reason and factual evidence.

I often do some research on my opponent. I look at his profile on social media or google his name. This gives me useful information. You can also identify him or her by asking a few questions.

Rule 3: Listen carefully to what your opponent is saying.

The dumbest thing I have done in debating is to give hasty responses without thoroughly listening to or reading carefully what my opponent communicates. It is crucial to understand his actual position. Be sure to consider the entire context of his point of view and how he interprets the terms he is using. Ask short questions on these things in order to completely understand every point he seems to be making.

Do not expect that your opponent will be swayed by your arguments. Often he will reject all your premises and conclusions, without providing any reasons for doing so. If you realize that you have lost a debate, do not be discouraged. We all lose debates. Take it as a learning experience that you can analyze for what you did wrong. This will sharpen your skills and make you increasingly more effective.

Here is an example of the unclear and incoherent writing you will frequently find in the arguments of some liberals:

> If government was limited only to responding if there was an apparent violation or threat, such a government would be small enough to be funded by voluntary donations. Not taxed into poverty people would have money left over to voluntary donate to Israel if they so choose, or do something else with their money. Next time you start a government don't have elections, don't have a legislature, and expressly forbid taxation.

After struggling to decipher this, we finally get the idea that he is saying a small government like Israel could exist by the voluntary contributions of individual Americans, and from this he illogically concludes that this is a good reason why the US government should not financially support Israel. The assumption here is that individual Americans would automatically step up to the task.

Many people, including us conservatives, have great trouble writing clearly but instead use bad grammar, incorrect spelling, and defective punctuation. Or they wander around in convoluted sentences, seldom communicating clear ideas. It is often maddening and time consuming to decode their remarks, and thus be able to respond properly.

Rule 4: Know your topic.

Of course, you cannot have a deep knowledge of every issue, but it is important to gain a reasonable amount of understanding of the subject you wish to debate. If you have not done this, you will be at a decided disadvantage. However, if you have done your homework, you will usually be able to expose and defeat your opponent's arguments without too much trouble, unless he is struggling to protect his ego. Why? Because most liberals do little or no serious research or thinking. They get most of their information from the mainstream media, television programs, and other leftist sources. They purposely choose those sources because they reinforce their preconceived notions.

Rule 5: Know and use the correct meanings of key terms.

Part of knowing your topic is to work with correct definitions. Liberals frequently depend on using tricky definitions that are constantly in flux to explain and justify their current positions and opinions. It is important not to allow them to do this, if possible.

The principal ideology of hard core liberals is the theory of moral relativism, and therefore they feel there are no such things as "true" definitions. For them, words mean what they emotionally want them to mean depending on circumstances. That means they may define words differently from you. The only way to handle this is to try getting them to agree on the meaning of words in the current situation.

Sometimes I resort to standard dictionaries like Merriam Webster's because liberal opponents often sense they will look silly disagreeing with the dictionary. But they may even evade this effort and jump to the insult stage. Liberals absolutely hate to be pinned down.

I suggest you never let your opponents get away with using tricky, Teflon definitions. In discussing climate change, do not allow them to resort to using expressions like "man-made climate change" as if it were a given because the real debate centers on whether or not man significantly impacts the climate. Do not accept terms like "climate collapse" or "climate emergency" or "climate crisis," because such terms are nothing but irrational scare tactics without any foundation in science. Do not permit your opponents to get away with calling an unborn baby a "fetus." Do not consent if they call gun control and gun confiscation "fair, sensible gun policy." To answer the Left's slippery definitions, see Chapter Three on the favorite slogans they use.

Rule 6: Always use your best English.

You do not have to use big words and fancy language to teach and influence people. In fact, it is usually more compelling if your language is simple, direct, clear, and straightforward. Still, if you make persistent errors in grammar, word usage, spelling, and punctuation, your opponent and your audience will no doubt consider you to be an uneducated simpleton and thus give your arguments less credence.

Rule 7: Never defend yourself.

Never defend yourself, your ideas, your arguments, your facts, your character, or your intelligence. When you are on the defensive, you are in an inferior, subordinate position and you'll always look bad no matter how brilliant your defense is. Always take the offensive, even if you just say, "I disagree with you." You may be able to put your opponent at a disadvantage by simply asking for proof.

Here is an example of the error in becoming defensive. This is the first part of a debate between Alan Dershowitz, a liberal Harvard law professor, and Norman Finkelstein, a radical, left-wing, political "scientist."

Subject: Dershowitz's new book The Case for Israel.
Actors: Alan Dershowitz (C/L), Normal Finkelstein (L)

Alan: My hope is that we can have a reasonable, serious debate, about the future, about the rights and wrongs . . . on both sides [Palestinian and Israeli] . . . I won't attack Mr. Finkelstein on his merits on his position. Let people read his book [*The Holocaust Industry*] and judge for themselves, and if he would refrain from personal attacks on me and let people judge the book [*The Case for Israel*] on its merits, I think we can move the ball forward and have a reasonable, serious debate . . . .

Norman: Well, I appreciate Alan Dershowitz's seriousness, at least in these remarks. I have no intention whatsoever in getting involved in an ad hominem debate with Mr. Dershowitz. I'm interested in the facts. I was asked to come in and discuss his new book . . . I read the book very carefully . . . I went to the footnotes. I went through it very carefully. And there's only one conclusion one can reach . . . And this is a scholarly judgment. It's not an ad hominem attack. Mr. Dershowitz has concocted a fraud, which amazingly, in large parts, he plagiarized from another fraud [Joan Peters, author of a 1984 book *From Time Immemorial*]. I found that pretty . . . shocking coming from a Harvard professor.[128]

So Finkelstein promises not to engage in personal insults and then, instead of addressing the issues, proceeds to do exactly that, calling Dershowitz a plagiarist, a fraud, and unqualified to teach at Harvard. Finkelstein pretends not to understand the meaning of the word plagiarist and ignores the fact that unfairly calling someone a plagiarist and a fraud is an ad hominem attack.

Finkelstein's arrogant, hypocritical attack is unfair because in his book Dershowitz quotes his sources accurately and gives them credit in his footnotes. As the debate continues, Finkelstein

---

128 Amy Goodman, "Norman Finkelstein vs Alan Dershowitz," *Democracy Now*, June 30, 2012, 49:22, https://www.youtube.com/watch?v=DeTpKASahAc.

continues the same tactic over and over. He also uses the tactics of virtue signaling and smug superiority.

Dershowitz makes his first mistake by even accepting to discuss his new book on the program Democracy Now, a known progressive news outlet, with the liberal host, Amy Goodman. It was clearly a calculated setup on the part of Democracy Now because Norman Finkelstein, a known leftist, anti-Semite, and Israel hater, was also invited as the debate opponent.

The result of all this is that Dershowitz was, of course, constantly on the defensive, and Finkelstein was the aggressor. Whenever someone spends his time defending himself, he invariably loses the debate.

Later, Harvard's president, Derek Bok, investigated the allegation and determined that no plagiarism had occurred.

Rule 8: Identify nonarguments.

When your liberal opponents make unsupported opinions, assertions, accusations, or engage in insults, ask them to give you proof of their claims in a rational argument, an argument that starts with reasonable premises and ends with an objective conclusion. Since liberals never have such an argument, they will normally continue with the same tactics as before or they will abruptly discontinue the discussion.

Yet if they do try to supply proof, almost always their arguments are illogical and easy to refute. Often they beat around the bush, change the subject, or make long nonsensical statements in a desperate effort to save face. Actually, all this can be quite hilarious and highly entertaining.

Rule 9: Insist on getting sources.

A request for sources can be very revealing. If your opponents try to support their contentions with facts or factoids, simply ask them for the sources of their information, always addressing them by name. You can do this in a sincere, inquiring way:

"Where can I find that information, Joe?" Progressives hate to give their sources because they seldom know where the information came from, or they have no sources other than their opinions and feelings.

But if they do give sources, you can be sure those sources will be from leftist provenances like the New York Times, the Washington Post, Politico, ABC, NBC, CBC, MSNBC, or CNN. Then you can remind them that all those references are leftist news sources and are not objective. They will not accept that, but they cannot refute it.

Sometimes, just asking for sources will end the debate, but make sure you have ready a list of

your sources (books, articles, documentaries, and so forth) on the topic at hand in case they ask

for them. Usually they will reject the validity of your sources, but if they do that, you have the

right to tell them that their sources are far more worthless.

Perhaps the most effective way to handle sources is to simply ask your interlocutors if they have ever read a book that disagrees with their contentions. If so, ask them to give you the title(s) of the book(s). I tell them that they now understand one side of the controversy, but would it not be honest and fair to hear the other side? When I have done this, they usually employ diversion or demand that you cite any works that support their side of the question.

Of course, if you are willing to endure a lot of torture, you can always buy books written by liberals. But I warn you that you'll get nothing but the same silly, repetitious, biased points of view as always. Besides, we've been hearing those opinions and their supporting "evidence" for decades and from every source imaginable, including novels, movies, TV series, liberal news reports, discussions forums, sitcoms, opinions of "learned" professors and other "experts," and so forth. A better plan would be to buy objective books written by conservatives. In these books you'll get honest, accurate descriptions of liberal positions, followed by excellent refutations.

Rule 10: Ask for specifics.

When your opponent makes general, all-encompassing statements or charges, do not address the general statements. When you try to characterize a general statement, you are simply providing a *conclusion* without constructing a real argument. Instead, ask him or her for precise details, saying perhaps, "What do you mean, specifically?"

It is usually hard for an indoctrinated person to come up with distinct examples because all he has learned are sweeping generalities as liberal talking points. Instead, he will probably stumble around trying to think of something. This indecision can be extremely comical, but it is not wise to point that out. Still, if he finally comes up with an example, then you can use your preparation to refute the point.

Rule 11: Ask your opponent what he would accept for both of you to come to an agreement.

To people monitoring your debate this question will seem like an honest effort on your part to reach a compromise with your rival. But it also puts the liberal on the defensive because he does not want to compromise but to search and destroy. He will look bad if he ends up saying, "Nothing you can say would make me agree with you."

Rule 12: Control your emotions, making sure your ideas are based on facts.

Some writers believe that it is quite appropriate to express emotion like indignation when your adversary makes self-evidently foolish attacks on things most people hold sacred such as the right to life of the unborn and the sacredness of the marriage bond. For example, Timothy Daughtry and Gary Casselman make this point:

> So when you're speaking on behalf of the mainstream about wrongs done by the radical left, it is fine to show passionate intensity appropriate to the situation. Show indignation at the injustice done to the taxpayers of the country. People need to know that you are one of them, that you are on their side, and that you share their frustrations. Think in terms of conviction, moral clarity, resolve, and a firm commitment to speaking the truth. But you never, ever want to appear angry or to be ruled by your emotions. Leave that to the liberals. Balance is the key.[129]

This is good advice, if you can do it. But we should remember that indignation is a form of anger, and it can be a double-edged sword, and achieving the right balance between "good" anger and "bad" anger is a chancy thing. I suggest that people who debate with leftists remain as cool and calm as possible because it is often difficult for us to determine how much indignation we are showing. Most important, your indignation should be genuine and based in facts.

When Candace Owens, the young black activist, appeared before a congressional hearing in September of 2019, her belief that the Democrats are responsible for black subservience was hatefully and falsely misrepresented by three liberal white women who ganged up on her. Candace was given time to respond and she refuted their contentions with passion and heated indignation. Her passion seemed to impress many at the hearing.[130]

The Left seems addicted to displays of indignation.[131]

---

129 Daughtry and Casselman, *Waking the Sleeping Giant*, p. 177.

130 Candace Owens, "Candace Owens at hearing on Confronting White Supremacy," *C-SPAN,* Sept. 20, 2019, 4:59, https://www.youtube.com/watch?v=0cUQqPxw3hc.

131 Mike Huckabee, "How CNN Tried And FAILED To Get The Drop On Dana Loesch," *FULL INTVW | Huckabee*, Feb. 29, 2020, 11:19, https://www.youtube.com/watch?v=B4JXtNTQZmI.

Rule 13: Remain calm when confronted by a very emotional person.

You cannot reason with an angry person because their strong feelings cloud their powers of reasoning, if they had any to begin with. Many liberals cherish anger as a matter of course and purposely use it to intimidate their "enemies." Their anger is a function of their character, not a reflection on yours. You might handle this by saying nothing while you wait for their fury to diminish. Or you might simply follow Christopher Hitchens and say, "What is your point?"[132]

Rule 14: Agree with your rival whenever you can.

Doing this will make everyone, perhaps even your opponent, think of you as a fair, reasonable person and thus strengthen your position. It may even disconcert your opponent. By this, I am not suggesting you should engage in coddling.

Rule 15: Know your own argument thoroughly.

This, of course, requires research and preparation. But even if you have made only a little preparation, you will probably still be in a superior position vis-à-vis your rival.

Rule 16: Make your opponent stay on the issue at hand.

Evasion, diversion, and deflection are the prime tactics of hard core liberals, and even trickle-down liberals, and they engage in those tactics frequently because they have no alternatives. There are many methods liberals employ to accomplish their diversions:

- changing the subject
- ignoring your points
- using insults
- attacking you on another subject
- declaring you are not qualified to judge

---

132 Christopher Hitchens, "I'm offended!" *Elias Tsigos*, Sept. 23, 2014, :20, https://www.youtube.com/watch?v=6pTbL7GYUuA.

- mentioning other people who disagree with you
- reminding you that some celebrated conservative held other views
- giving long, convoluted answers with big words that may sound profound but mean nothing
- attacking your grammar and punctuation instead of trying to make an argument
- monopolizing the discussion

When they use any form of evasion, you must insist that they get back on track. You can say over and over, "Let's stick to the subject" or "That's another question" or "What's your argument?" or something like that.

Now about monopolizing the conversation. They do this because they know or sense that they have nothing valid to contribute to the discussion, and if they let you talk for one single minute, you might produce evidence and facts they cannot answer. So, they must quickly evade the issues and silence you at all cost. How can you stop them? Well, if they were in the same room, you might try to put a muzzle on them, but that might turn out to be counterproductive. All kidding aside, what can we do?

Here is one suggestion. You might raise your hand and say, "Stop! You are monopolizing the conversation. It's my turn now." President Trump does something like this when liberal reporters never stop asking loaded questions. He raises a hand at them and says, "Excuse me, excuse me, excuse me, excuse me," or "Be quiet, be quiet, be quiet," and then he continues his message. In one short segment he might do this many times.

Staying on topic is especially hard in debates on social media. Often when two people are discussing an important issue, other people—sometimes many people—will jump in to make comments, some agreeing with you and others disagreeing. It is not unusual for those people to bring up arguments and facts on completely different issues.

This can be very disconcerting and overwhelming. If you try to respond to every opponent, the main issue will soon become lost in a morass of conflicting opinions, and no one will get anywhere. If you want to stay on topic, I suggest that you ignore all the comments made except those given by your original opponent. You can do this by mentioning his or her name at the beginning of each of your replies.

Rule 17: Avoid any kind of trickery, rudeness, condescension, vulgarity, or ad hominem insults. In other words, strictly shun all of the deceptive tactics of the Left outlined in this book.

I have been disappointed to see some conservatives and moderates use name-calling and insults in personal discussions. In general, they might promote good policies and principles, but they sometimes foolishly allow excessive emotion to lead them to fall into one of the Left's most egregious tactics—insults, which are a form of evasion. And in the process, they lose the debate because they have lowered themselves to the level of the very people they desire to defeat.

If we engage in any of these kinds of negative behavior, we will leave ourselves open to attack from our opponent, and we will lose the respect of those monitoring the debate. If we use these tactics with friends or relatives, we may well lose their love and respect forever.

I believe there is one exception to using ad hominem attacks. It is fair to use a reasonable amount of name-calling—but avoiding vulgarity and obscenity—when you characterize leftist groups or public figures *with whom you are not debating personally.* You must make sure, of course, that these attacks are based on facts, not only on opinion.

When liberals insult me personally, calling me ignorant, stupid, uneducated, evil, or a hater of mankind, I am pleased because I know my opponent finally realizes he has lost the debate and has nothing more to contribute. I try to ignore the insults and ask my interlocutor if he has an argument buried there in all his comments.

In direct social gatherings, there is an especially good method of dealing with an attacker in Rusty Humphries's interesting book, *7 Ways To Win Political Debates with Your Liberal Family and Friends*. Rusty calls this method "Social Proof." The other people at the gathering will be witnessing the discussion and, wanting to be happy and enjoy the meeting, they do not like angry confrontations. Because of that, they will be on your side when you are confronted with an angry attacker if you remain calm, nice, and pleasant, and thereby diffuse the situation. This will also tend to disconcert and embarrass your attacker.[133]

Once, when I did not understand this principle, I was approached and directly attacked by a fellow professor at a faculty meeting. She said, "The trouble with you, Ken, is that you have to classify and categorize everything."

I responded by saying, "The trouble with you, Jackie, is that no one ever pays any attention to anything you say." My statement was true but very insulting. The result was that all the other teachers at the meeting turned their backs on me and walked away. I had made everyone feel uncomfortable. Actually, Jackie's accusation was foolish because it is the normal job of literature professors to analyze and classify the literary works they teach, but she made the accusation for personal reasons.

However, that fact did nothing to save me from the opprobrium of my colleagues, and her original personal attack was completely ignored by them. What I should have said was something like this: "Thank you, Jackie, I'll try to keep that in mind."

If you employ personal attacks, most people will interpret that as a clear sign that you have no valid contentions. Instead, discuss only what they say and do, never who they are. The temptation to

133 Rusty Humphries, *7 Ways To Win Political Debates with Your Liberal Family and Friends*, pp. 15-19.

reply with personal attacks is so great during the storm of controversy, that good people can easily fall into that trap without realizing it.

Rule 18: Watch for three basic weaknesses in your opponent's position: false assumptions, hypocrisy, and contradictions.

Because their definitions are always in flux and their philosophy is based on nothing good, leftists contradict themselves constantly. If we can expose those contradictions and inconsistencies, we can disarm their nonarguments quickly. Here is a real-life mini debate illustrating liberal contradictions:

Subject: Loving everyone.
Actors: Margo (L), Maurice (C)

Margo: Oh! I'm sooo happy!

Maurice: Why is that, Margo?

Margo: I just love everyone. Absolutely everyone!

Maurice: Everyone?

Margo: Yes, just everyone!

Maurice: Does that include Donald Trump?

Margo: Yuck! I hate Donald Trump! I totally hate that freak!

Maurice: But why?

Margo: Because he's so full of hate! He hates everybody!

Maurice: Ah! I get it. You love everyone except those you hate.

Analysis: It is easy to see how Margo has contradicted herself and exposed the shallowness of her proclaimed love.

Rule 19: Use humor whenever possible.

Even though it is probably not wise to act like a stand-up comedian, you can use humor to your advantage if you ironically accept that their insults might have some validity. For example, if your opponent accuses you of being a flat-earther, you might say, "Oh, the earth isn't flat?" Or if he says you are stupid, you might reply, "Well, my wife calls me that all the time" or "That's what my psychology teacher said before I got the highest grade in his class" or "My gosh! That IQ test must have been wrong." It doesn't hurt to be a bit of a joker before you ask your disputer to provide an argument.

Rule 20: Do not accept or use arguments based entirely on strong emotions.

When debaters use emotional arguments involving *ad hominem*, they are often trying to manipulate you and the emotions of the people witnessing the exchange. Many people who use this technique do not actually realize they are doing it. However, intelligent people will see through such manipulation and resent it.

For example, a person who says, "Have you no heart?" or "Have you no shame?" is employing an emotional response without substance. There are also many other ways to argue emotionally. President Obama was using an argument based entirely on feelings when, as a part of public statements supporting gun control, he surrounded himself with suffering victims of gun violence and their tearful relatives to "prove" we needed more gun control.

Some people, almost always liberals, defend their opinions as if they were the absolute truth. Often they become vehement, antagonistic, and express uncontrolled anger. They make loud, angry, insistent pronouncements and become repetitive and overbearing, never letting their opponent voice an opposing opinion. Such people inadvertently reveal the weakness of their positions because they depend on noise and browbeating to support their points.

They may even seem completely immune or hostile to rational arguments and empirical evidence. Usually these people do no or little serious reading and reflection. It may be best to let them rant in a vacuum, for it is unlikely that they will ever change their opinions, unless some real-life events force them to do so.

Other trickle-down liberals get their marching orders from

leftist teachers or Alinskyesque radicals. Their prime tactic is to muzzle themselves and not talk at all. The silly theory behind this seems to be that reasoning with conservatives only serves to legitimize conservative positions. There are now so many groups using this tactic that it must be a strategy they received from a central, organized source.

Rule 21: Do not be impressed with opponents who try to discombobulate you with high-sounding rhetoric, big words, and doctored statistics.

Liberals who have some education are often clever with language, but their arguments are typically devoid of substance. In criticizing some of the dumb decisions made by his colleagues on the Supreme Court, Justice Antonin Scalia called their work "showy profundities." The following examples of oxymoron also describe many liberal arguments:

- incoherent profundities
- deep superficialities
- weighty inconsistencies
- wise stupidities

Most arguments boil down to one or two simple points, but those points may be lost in verbiage or camouflaged by ridiculous, semisophisticated rhetoric. To make sure you understand what your opponents actually mean, you could ask, "Can you say that in a different way? I don't understand what you're getting at." Or you might ask, "Please explain that to me again in simple terms." The liberal will often find it difficult to do that, especially since they have no argument.

Rule 22: Avoid using links within a thread on social media.

In my opinion, this is a tactic you should avoid. I believe that in a debate on social media, it is a waste of time to think you have responded effectively to an opponent's argument by giving a link to another site. I believe people seldom pay attention to such links. It is much more effective to summarize the contents of a link directly in the current thread. I have noted that both liberals and conservatives employ this poor tactic.

Rule 23: Try using these techniques when dealing with severely brainwashed, politically correct people on social media.

Technique one.

When brainwashed liberals make a number of unsupported claims in one post, take on the most important claim only. Why? Because they cannot deal with several responses and they will usually reply to only part of what you say anyway. In this way, you can save a great deal of time giving them lessons on things they should know if they did any honest research.

In the case of especially arrogant and resistant people, it will save you a lot of time and frustration if you use two simple tactics: disagreement and contradiction.

Disagreement:
"I disagree with you."
"I don't see it that way."
"That's just an opinion."
"I don't believe that."

Contradiction:
"No, that's incorrect."
"No, he did not say that."
"That isn't true."

If they demand that you explain yourself or provide proof, reply that you are simply giving your opinion. This will save you hours of time because these people won't accept your responses anyway. Die-hard liberals pride themselves on believing that they alone have the ultimate truth and that most people (usually their friends) agree with them. Therefore, it is often disconcerting for them to see someone who dares to disagree. They may even strain a gut trying to convince you. See strategy 2, given in chapter four, for an example of this tactic in operation.

Technique two.

Probably the most effective way to debate with liberals or anyone else, and still avoid conflict, is to employ *questions* rather than *assertions* or explanatory comments. To do this properly requires a lot of skill, but it can be learned by anyone. For example, if your opponent badmouths America because the Founding Fathers were "racists and rapists," it would probably be a waste of time to give him a lesson on the founding of America. Instead, ask him detailed questions, one at a time, as to why he feels the Founders were racists and rapists. You will find that it is very unlikely he will be able to give evidence proving his claims.

The following section goes more into detail concerning the question technique.

Rule 24: Use the Socratic Method of Questioning in debates.

The Socratic Method of Questioning is a powerful tool for defeating the arguments of hard core liberals. The following rules are found in Peter Kreeft's book, *Socratic Logic*, "Debating with the Difficult Person."

1. Find out exactly what your opponent is saying by asking—if necessary—"What are you saying?"
2. Be sure you understand by asking for clear definitions of terms. You might ask, "What, exactly, do you mean by . . . ?"
3. Clarify by repeating back his ideas in your own words.
4. Either explore his premises or his conclusions. The latter is better because a realization of unnecessary *conclusions* might make him reevaluate his premises in private.
5. Do not highlight his "logical fallacies" per se. He must conclude those for himself.

6. Offer alternative conclusions.
7. By analyzing his conclusions, you are using *reductio ad absurdum.*
8. Do not present this analysis as if he did not know it, but give him the idea that you realize he already knew the logical absurdity. This is rather difficult to do, but if you can achieve it, it will allow him to save face and soothe his ego.
9. Give the difficult person alternative options (as many as possible) so he has a choice.
10. Make sure the options are constructive rather than negative so he does not feel destroyed. If he feels destroyed anywhere along in this, he will still cling to his false conclusions.
11. Let him decide which alternative is best.
12. If he chooses a false option, you may have to probe further with questions.[134]

Here are some real-life mini discussions involving the Socratic Method:

Subject: Translation (Translation is the religious belief that someone can be instantly changed from mortality to immortality because of righteousness.)
Actors: Jim (C), George (L), Naomi (L)

Jim: Is there a cure for old age?

George: Yeah, death.

Naomi: Getting translated.

Jim: Naomi, have you seen that happen recently?

Naomi: Still working on it myself.

Analysis: Naomi evades the question because she does not know the answer. Jim does not press it because he believes Naomi

---

134 Peter Kreeft, *Socratic Logic*, pp. 300-355.

is a decent person and the answer is not really important. But the exchange tends to discredit Naomi's observation.

Subject: Voting for the lesser of two evils.
Actors: Greta (L), Mark (C)

Greta has posted a big picture on Facebook that repeats twenty times, "Voting for the lesser of two evils is still evil."

Mark: Greta, what is the lesser of two evils?

Greta: It's when both candidates are evil but you decide to vote for the one who is less evil. Since you decide to vote for him you are still supporting evil.

Mark: Okay, but how do you decide which is less evil?

Greta: You pay attention to what they say and do.

Mark: That seems reasonable. But if you don't vote for the lesser evil, doesn't that improve the chances of the greater evil being elected?

Greta: No, not really. I would vote for a third candidate who is not evil.

Mark: What if that candidate has absolutely no chance of being elected? Would you still vote for him?

Greta: Yes, because we must always support the best candidate we can find. It's the noble thing to do.

Mark: I agree. Idealistically, it's the most honorable thing to do. But in the real world of dog-eat-dog politics, wouldn't you be throwing away your vote, and in the long run, wouldn't that help the greater evil be elected because you declined to vote for the person who was less evil?

Greta: Well, that does seem logical. I'm just expressing my worthless opinion.

Mark: Don't say that. We all have problems with our opinions sometimes.

Subject: Gun control
Actors: Andrew (L), Robert (C)

Andrew: We must stop all these gun killings!

Robert: How can we do that, Robert?

Andrew: By passing comprehensive gun control legislation.

Robert: What does that mean?

Andrew: You know, laws restricting who can get guns.

Robert: Don't we already have hundreds of those laws?

Andrew: Some, yes, but not enough. We need to pass more so there are fewer guns available.

Robert: But won't that infringe on the Second Amendment rights of law-abiding Americans?

Andrew: Well, we must all make sacrifices for the common good.

Robert: But criminals don't obey the laws. Won't they still get guns?

Andrew: How can they? There won't be any guns for them to get.

Robert: But in areas where guns are most controlled, like in Chicago and New York, they still seem to get guns, don't they?

Andrew: Yes, but it's because they steal guns from relatives who bought guns legally.

Robert: That's true, but whose fault is that?

Andrew: The person who steals guns.

Robert: So, are you saying that legal gun owners have no responsibility to lock up their guns?

Andrew: Well, the disturbed criminal can always find a way.

Robert: That's true, but doesn't that mean the sick person or criminal can get guns on the black market?

Andrew: That's a myth. The black market doesn't exist.

Robert: How do you know that?

Andrew: It just doesn't, that's all.

Subject: Global warming
Actors: Madge (L), Leonard (C)

Madge: We must stop man-made climate change because in twelve years it will destroy all life on earth.

Leonard: What do you mean by climate change?

Madge: What? It's obvious. The earth is heating up fast.

Leonard: But the earth has always gone through periods of heating and cooling. What makes our days any different?

Madge: It's much worse now because of man-made carbon dioxide emissions.

Leonard: Yet in the past thousands of years, CO2 levels were much higher than now, long before the industrial revolution. So what makes things so much worse now?

Madge: It's the rate. It's happening faster now.

Leonard: What is the proper rate of change?

Madge: Um, well, I don't know, but climate scientists say it is.

Leonard: What climate scientists?

Madge: In a big study, a consensus of 97% of climate scientists agree that the planet is dangerously heating. If we don't do something radical right now, we'll all die in twelve years.

Leonard: Have you read that study?

Madge: No, not yet.

Leonard: You should read it. It's a bogus study designed by climate alarmists to propagandize their agenda. But let me ask you, is truth in science based on consensus or on empirical, factual data?

Madge: On a consensus.

Leonard: What about the 31,000 real climate scientists who say there is no proof that climate change is an existential threat?

Madge: What 31,000?

Leonard: You'll find out if you research it.

Subject: Free speech
Actors: Julia (C), Albert (L), Marco (L)

Julia: I think Obama was the worst president in American history.

Albert: That's terrible. That's nothing but hate speech.

Marco: Yeah, Julia, you're a moron.

Julia: Albert, what is hate speech?

Marco: Whatever you say is hate speech.

Albert: Julia, it's when you say bad things about a great leader or anyone else.

Julia: Are you saying I have no right to give my opinion?

Marco: Your opinions are obviously stupid and so are you.

Albert: Of course you have a right to your opinions, but when you disparage people, especially good people, you are creating unnecessary conflict, causing division, setting a bad example for innocent children, and even hurting yourself.

Marco: Yeah, you're a bad, nasty person.

Julia: Albert, what if that person is lying, stealing, or undermining the Constitution? Should I just ignore that?

Albert: No, you should vote him or her out of office.

Julia: You're right, Albert. I should vote against them, but one person has little influence. What's wrong with me exposing the evil person and getting others to oppose him? What's wrong with me trying to inform others, to maybe starting a movement?

Marco: There you go again, spreading hate and division!

Albert: I see your point, but why can't you be positive about it and simply say the person made honest mistakes. Not everyone has bad motives.

Julia: Oh, I see, Albert. If I agree with you I'm using free speech properly, but if I disagree with you, I'm using hate speech. Is that right?

Albert: Well, no. Well, maybe.

Marco: No! If you say what offends me, you're using hate speech. Dumb broad!

(neither Julia nor Albert say more.)

Analysis: Note how Julia challenges Albert's conclusions (no right to my opinion) and asks for definitions of terms (hate speech). At the same time she ignores Marco's insults as if they were not worthy of response. To keep the focus on Albert, she addresses him by name so we'll know she's not talking to Marco.

Subject: Vaccines
Actors: Rachel (C), Andrea (L)

Andrea: Everyone should get the vaccines. They are safe and effective.

Rachel: How do you know they're safe and effective?

Andrea: Crap! Everybody knows that. It's common knowledge. Smart people know that.

Rachel: Well, I guess I'm not smart. But truth is not determined by what is popular or who is dumb or smart. What facts prove they are safe and effective?

Andrea: Well, let's see. They've saved millions and millions of lives all over the world.

Rachel: How do we know they've saved millions of lives?

Andrea: The studies, all of them, have verified that.

Rachel: What studies?

Andrea: Studies done by scientific experts.

Rachel: What experts?

Andrea: Experts who study vaccines, like virologists and immunologists.

Rachel: What virologists and immunologists?

Andrea: Crap! I don't know. I don't memorize their names.

Rachel: Do they work for the drug companies?

Andrea: Oh yeah, that's right, most of them.

Rachel: In't that a conflict of interest when the experts work for the very companies who

profit from the sale of vaccines?

Andrea: Oh no, they have the people's best interest at heart, not profits.

Rachel: I see. They are completely altruistic. What convincing studies have they done to prove the great value of vaccines?

Andrea: Oh, lots of them. Everybody knows that. Just google it.

Rachel: Can you name one study?

Andrea: Um, well no, not really.

Rachel: You're not at fault. The fact is, there has never been a large double-blind placebo-controlled study of vaccines. The drug companies like Merck and health authorities like the CDC have refused to make such a study. So what proof is there that vaccines are safe and effective?

Andrea: That question is just stupid and not worth answering. Everybody knows for a fact and by experience that vaccines are the great miracle of modern medicine! They have saved untold millions of human lives!

Rachel: Where is the proof of that?

Analysis: "Everybody knows" is not factual evidence. Andrea is depending on emotion and politically correct notions popularized by drug company ads, the media, the health agencies, and medical experts.

Subject: Immigration
Actors: Shem (L), Annie (L), Brigitte (C)

Shem: America has always been the great melting pot. Remember what it says on the Statue of Liberty about "Give me your poor, your tired, your huddled masses." That's proof we should welcome here all the needy people who want to come here.

Brigitte: Shem, that's Emma Lazarus's poem of 1883, not a legal document.

Shem: But that's why America is so unique and great. We should let anyone come here who wants to. So, Brigitte, why do you conservatives oppose that so violently?

Annie: Yeah, why? That's so racist! But, Shem, I don't think America has ever been great.

Brigitte: Annie, if America is not great, why do so many millions of migrants risk their lives to get here?

Annie: Uh, I'm not sure. Wait! To escape tyranny in their own countries.

Brigitte: Well, Annie, that's only what the liberal media claims. But Shem, why do you support open borders so fervently?

Shem: Out of love. To help the poor, the suffering, the precious little children.

Brigitte: That really sounds noble. You're obviously a good person. Do you also love poor and suffering Americans and the 553,000 homeless Americans living on the streets?

Shem: Of course. I love everyone.

Annie: Which is more than Brigitte does.

Brigitte: Okay, Shem. Then why do you want to support policies that would bring them more poverty and suffering?

Shem: What? How am I doing that?

Brigitte: Well, if the immigrants are poor, they'll need food stamps, handouts, and jobs, won't they?

Annie: And they deserve them. They're HUMAN BEINGS after all!

Shem: Stands to reason.

Brigitte: And who pays for that public assistance? And who can't get jobs because the illegal immigrants get so many of them?

Shem: The Mexican immigrants only do work that Americans won't do, like harvesting crops in the fields.

Brigitte: But it was a Mexican who fixed my dryer, and he admitted he was undocumented. Also, Mexican teams put a roof on our bank down the street and huge signs on our local market. I've seen Hispanics do all kinds of work here. They don't even speak English. I had to use my bad Spanish on some of them.

Shem: America is rich and can afford it. The new migrants pay taxes and contribute vast amounts of money to the economy.

Brigitte: Are we rich enough to support the hundreds of millions who yearn to come here? I think not. And why do you say they pay a lot of taxes? The people who are at the bottom of the economic ladder pay no taxes. The IRS says that those below 47% in income pay no income taxes at all.

Shem: But everybody knows that migrants have made wonderful contributions to this country.

Annie: Yeah, everybody knows it except Brigitte.

Brigitte: Shem, are you talking about legal or illegal immigrants?

Shem: Both.

Brigitte: Listen. Before 1914, most migrants were legal and made great contributions by working and struggling to improve their lot. But after 1914, when our welfare programs started, we suddenly got a huge flood of illegals entering the country seeking handouts. Don't you think we should take care of our own people first by helping them qualify for better jobs?

Annie: That's the dumbest thing I've ever heard! It's selfish, cruel, and just inhuman! You damn conservatives!

Analysis: The debate speaks for itself.

CONCLUSION

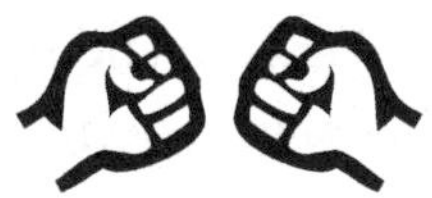

America is the world's greatest experiment in freedom. It is mankind's bright light of hope. It is the only true bulwark on earth against slavery, brutality, poverty, evil, and despotism. It is the only power that can stop the insatiable lust of ignorant, selfish, and greedy men to rule in global tyranny. America is the ultimate test as to whether or not human beings are good enough, wise enough, and capable enough to govern themselves.

America is great for two basic reasons: the essential goodness of its people and the most advanced, effective, and remarkable form of government ever known. This government was created by our inspired Founding Fathers and is comprised in the US Constitution. The governmental structure of no other nation can begin to compare, neither those existing now or those of the past.

Of course, from the very beginning of this nation, critics living in the US have found fault with their own country for not being perfect. Some of these people are what we might call the loyal opposition, who see real weaknesses and genuinely want to make things better. We would do well to listen to them.

But other accusers of a different stripe have abounded. These people are bent on looking only for weaknesses and never seem able to see the good. For them, nothing is ever good enough and so they arrogantly conspire to remake America in their own image. These blind seekers of trouble never acknowledge or are grateful for the marvelous blessings of freedom and the great privileges their homeland has given them. Thus, they foolishly strive to overthrow America and its traditions and replace them with an insane Utopia which they imagine to be more desirable.

These dangerous cynics have increased in number and boldness over the course of American history, and today the most virulent of these detractors are called liberals, progressives, and leftists. Inspired by Darwinism, Marxism, and socialism, these people espouse an ideology that has always been disastrous wherever it has been tried.

These destroyers have adopted the evil doctrine of relativism, and their primary effort is to accomplish their goals by any and every means possible. Those means include lying, anger, hate, misrepresentation, contradictions, discrediting, vilifying, manipulation, bullying, and murder. Their personal motives are to gain power, fame, influence, and wealth.

Therefore, in order to frustrate their designs and stop them, we must go on the offensive by exposing and opposing their beliefs, their practices, and their policies. For the sake of liberty we must win this war between good and evil. For the sake of our posterity and for the freedom of all nations we cannot afford to lose this fight. Our love for our country and the blessings it provides will give us the power to do this.

The purpose of this book is to help loyal, patriotic Americans accomplish this victory.

APPENDIX A:

List of Conservative Commentators (Partly Following Conservapedia)

- Beck, Glenn (American conservative political commentator, radio host, and television producer)
- Bennett, Kaitlin (reporter for InfoWars)
- Bongino, Dan (host of the Dan Bongino Show and Fox News contributor)
- Buttrill, Jason (chief researcher and writer for The Glenn Beck Program)
- Carlson, Tucker (host of Tucker Carlson Tonight, Fox News, engaging and effective debater
against leftists)
- Chaffetz, Jason (former Republican member of the House, now a news analyst)
- Chen, Lauren (reporter for BlazeTV)
- Chen, Melissa (Asian critic of postmodernism)
- Clarke, David (pro-Trump commentator, former sheriff of Milwaukee County)
- Colter, Ann (author and commentator)

- Concha, Joe (reporter for The Hill)
- Condell, Pat (anti-Muslim commentator)
- Dice, Mark (satirical analyst who delights in exposing Fake News)
- Dobbs, Lou (anchor of Lou Dobbs Tonight on Fox News)
- D'Souza, Dinesh (author of The Big Lie, film maker, speaker)
- Elder, Larry (host of the Larry Elder Show, for the Epoch Times)
- Farage, Nigel (British creator of Brexit, anti-Muslim commentator)
- Gabriel, Brigitte (smart, outspoken, anti-radical Muslim activist)
- Geller, Pam (smart, outspoken anti-radical Muslim activist)
- Gorka, Dr. Sebastian (commentator who served as a Deputy Assistant to the President in the administration of President Donald Trump)
- Gutfeld, Greg (entertaining and fervent host of The Five on Fox News)
- Gonzales, Sara (humorous analyst on The Blaze)
- Gowdy, Trey (Republican legislator)
- Hannan, Daniel (British member of the European Parliament against socialism)
- Hannity, Sean (host of Hannity on Fox News, excellent debater)
- Hanson, Victor Davis (American classicist, military historian, columnist and farmer)
- Heller, Tony (brilliant expert on climate change, debunks the claims of climate alarmists)
- Hilton, Steve (host of The Next Revolution, Fox News)
- Hopkins, Katie (bold, outrageous conservative British commentator)
- Huckabee, Mike (candidate in the US Republican presidential primaries in both 2008 and 2016, currently an insightful political analyst)

- Hughes, Brittany (commentator for Reality Check, MRCTV, smart, vigorous, outspoken)
- Ingraham, Laura (insightful host of The Ingraham Angle on Fox News, well-spoken and confident)
- Jones, Alex (head of InfoWars.com. A little aggressive in manner, but usually right. Anti-Muslim, anti-globalist)
- Klavan, Andrew (brilliant commentator who hosts his own show)
- Knowles, Michael (brilliant, informed speaker and analyst)
- Lahren, Tomi (commentator who hosted Tomi on TheBlaze, where she gained notice for her short video segments called "final thoughts," in which she frequently criticized liberal politics)
- Ledger, Graham (insightful host of the Daily Ledger)
- Levin, Mark R. (strong, brilliant constitutional radio talk host against global warming, etc.)
- Loesch, Dana (intelligent defender of gun rights for the NRA)
- Malkin, Michelle (discerning analyst and author, founded Hot Air, against illegal immigration)
- Murray, Douglas (a Brit against open borders and diversity)
- Noir, Colion (an American civil rights activist, lawyer, and host of the web series NOIR)
- O'Reilly, Bill (American journalist, author, and former television host, author of No Spin Zone and other books)
- Ott, Scott (runs Scrapple Face, satirizes news from a conservative viewpoint)
- Owens, Candace (young black woman who exposes the racism of the Democrats, creator of Blexit, trying to free blacks from Democrat tyranny)
- Paul, Rand (Libertarian senator and author of *Government Bullies*)
- Paul, Ron (retired Libertarian senator, author)
- Peterson, Jordan Bernt (Canadian clinical psychologist and

professor of psychology at the University of Toronto, defender of free speech.

- Pirro, Judge Jeanine (witty, vigorous American television host, author, former New York judge, prosecutor, and politician, currently the host of Fox News Channel's Justice with Judge Jeanine)
- Regan, Trish (sincere, discerning news analyst for Fox News)
- Salvi, Alex (reporter on After Hours for One America News Network)
- Savage, Michael (host of The Savage Nation, brilliant, aggressive analyst)
- Shapiro, Ben (Jewish political commentator, public speaker, author, and lawyer, somewhat flaky and politically correct)
- Sopo, Giancarlo (staff writer for Blaze TV)
- Southern, Lauren (Canadian analyst on The Rebel, cultural Libertarian)
- Sowell, Thomas (brilliant economist and commentator)
- Spencer, Robert (anti-radical Muslim author and commentator)
- Steyn, Mark (humorous Canadian author and cultural commentator)
- Varney, Stuart (British-born, American talk show host and conservative political commentator for Fox News and the Fox Business Network, hosts MyTake, FoxBusiness)
- Voight, Jon (conservative actor)
- Warner, Bill, PhD (speaker, author, human rights activist, anti-Muslim expert)
- Watters, Jesse (American political commentator on Fox News Channel, frequently appeared on the political talk show The O'Reilly Factor, known for his man-on-the-street interviews, featured in his segment of the show, "Watters' World," member of The Five)
- Watson, Paul Joseph (British YouTuber, defender of England against Islam, member of the New Right)

- Weaver, Millie (analyst for Millennial Millie.com, reporter for InfoWars)
- Wheeler, Liz (perceptive analyst on Tipping Point, OAN)
- Whittle, Bill (American conservative political commentator and YouTuber, made videos for PJ Media as the presenter of Afterburner and The Firewall, and as cohost of Right Angle with Stephen Green and Scott Ott, his former fellow co-hosts of Trifecta.)
- Witt, Will (He now creates online content for PragerU and helps inspire young people worldwide to fight for the values they believe in.)
- Yiannopoulos, Milo (British political commentator, polemicist, public speaker, author and activist, former editor for Breitbart News, describes himself as a "cultural Libertarian.")

APPENDIX B:

List of Conservative and Semiconservative News Sources (Following Conservapedia)

- American Thinker (daily internet publication devoted to the thoughtful exploration of issues of importance to Americans)
- Bizpac Review (conservative news and opinion website)
- The Blaze (information and opinion web site, blog and TV show which has combined with Conservative Review TV[CRTV] to create Blaze Media)
- Breitbart News (breaks some big stories and exposes liberal deceit, takes a strong conservative stance on most issues, including social issues)
- Campus Reform (an activist and news website focused on the issues of student indoctrination in America's colleges and universities)
- Chicks on the Right (a trio of conservative women who also have a radio program)
- Christian Broadcasting Network (CBN) (a division of the American Family News Network, reporting on general news with liberal selection bias)

- Christian Science Monitor (against mainstream media bias)
- Conservative News and Views (relatively new, covers a variety of conservative issues but mostly politics)
- Conservative Review (takes a very strong and consistent conservative stance on immigration and border security and does not hesitate to criticize Republicans for their failure on that issue, among others)
- The Conservative Treehouse (a ragtag bunch of conservative misfits)
- CNS News (uniquely informative news across all issues, including social ones, a top-quality news site in every respect)
- Daily Caller (DC) (a conservative news website co-founded by journalist and media personality Tucker Carlson)
- The Daily Ledger (American daily newspaper published in Canton, Illinois, related to One America News Network)
- The Daily Signal (publication of The Heritage Foundation)
- The Daily Wire (a news and opinion website founded by Ben Shapiro, very popular)
- Federalist, The (a division of the American Family News Network, reporting on general news with liberal selection bias)
- First Things (a conservative website founded by Richard John Neuhaus to promote public philosophy and oppose secular ideology)
- Fox News (FNC's primetime hosts [as of 2017] are strongly conservative and pro-Trump. In general, it takes a slightly more conservative stance than the rest of the mainstream media and covers stories that the MSM chooses to skim over or not to report on. However, it still has some left-leaning bias, is run by the globalist Murdoch family, and it has censored many conservatives and downplays the social issues.)
- Free Republic (an online message board for independent, grass-roots conservatism on the web)

- FrontPage Magazine (an online American conservative political magazine)
- Gateway Pundit (tremendous writing, with a rapier wit, and the national leader in breaking honest news on big stories like the events in Ferguson, Missouri)
- The Heritage Foundation (an American conservative think tank based in Washington, D.C., primarily geared towards public policy)
- The Hill (terrific source of news from Washington, D.C., usually without liberal bias although its comment section is overwhelmed with snide anti-Trump and anti-conservative comments by irrational liberal posters)
- Hot Air (Founded by Michelle Malkin in 2006, Hot Air typically links to other stories, often with a neoconservative emphasis rather than socially conservative.)
- Human Events (founded as a conservative magazine in 1944)
- Judicial Watch (public interest group, investigates and prosecutes government corruption)
- Legal Insurrection (a popular conservative law blog)
- LifeNews.com (conservative but not pro-life enough)
- LifeSiteNews (has lots of abortion-related stories, and prioritizes them well, but is not critical enough of politicians who pretend to be pro-life)
- LifeZette (a conservative magazine founded and run by Laura Ingraham)
- Live Action (also known as Live Action Films, a leading new media, investigative, and educational organization founded by Lila Rose and committed to the protection and respect of all human life)
- Louder with Crowder (Steven Crowder hosts a conservative news YouTube channel that has been wrongly banned by liberals for wrong-think.)
- Media Research Center (MRC) (a conservative media watchdog group)

- Moonbattery (a website to discuss all the craziness coming from moonbats, referring to liberals, progressives, or leftists)
- The New American Magazine (consistently conservative news and commentary; emphasizes issues related to globalism and national sovereignty and the left-wing push for world government that even many conservative outlets choose not to cover)
- NewsBusters (affiliated with CNS News, insightful, original, and good across all issues, exposes liberal deceit well)
- Newsmax (a growing enterprise, publishes a monthly magazine, maintains a website, and offers a cable television channel called NewsMax TV)
- New York Post (a conservative tabloid newspaper owned by Rupert Murdoch, who also owns Fox News)
- One America News Network (OAN) (best known for its news reports, which are objective and straightforward and its conservative talk shows, The Daily Ledger, hosted by Graham Ledger, and Tipping Point, hosted by Liz Wheeler)
- OneNewsNow.com (a division of the American Family News Network, reporting on general news with liberal selection bias)
- Orange County Register (the newspaper for the region that once propelled Ronald Reagan to become the governor of California, and then the President of the United States)
- Pajamas Media (pjmedia.com) (a conservative opinion and commentary collaborative blog, founded in 2004)
- Power Line (exposed "Rathergate")
- Project Veritas (an American activist group that uses hidden cameras to uncover liberal bias and corruption)
- Reason.com (a Libertarian-minded news website that promotes free markets)
- RedState (unhelpful or worse on social issues, such as piling on against William Todd Akin amid the media bullying, and very anti-Trump during the 2016 presidential election.

Otherwise, a decent source for conservative news and commentary)

- The Right Scoop (a conservative media news blog)
- Rush Limbaugh (one of the most well-known conservative broadcasters)
- Sky News Australia (an Australian 24-hour cable and satellite news channel available on the Foxtel and Optus Television subscription platforms)
- Stars and Stripes (a newspaper aimed at military members and US Armed Forces)
- Townhall.com (covering breaking news, US news, world news, investigative reporting, politics, political humor, conservative opinions, and more)
- Twitchy (a news and Twitter-tracking website, founded by Michelle Malkin)
- Voice of America (good sometimes)
- Voice of Europe (focuses on Europe, particularly immigration and EU-related stories from a conservative standpoint)
- The Wall Street Journal (often runs conservative editorials, and news but does not have as much bias as other mainstream media sites)
- Washington Examiner (has several strongly conservative commentators and news, is mostly free of liberal bias, though exceptions exist in both categories)
- Washington Times (conservative news source from the nation's capital)
- wattsupwiththat (a blog exposing the global warming hoax and other liberal falsehoods masquerading as science)
- WorldNetDaily (WND) (an excellent conservative news and commentary source, but still allowed a column that savaged William Todd Akin.)
- Western Journal/Conservative Tribune (highly popular conservative news outlet)

APPENDIX C:
The Rogues' Gallery of BigLeft Organizations

Another major tactic of the Left is to establish permanent, subversive, secret or semisecret societies, organizations, and think tanks to further anti-American, leftist causes. The members of these organizations meet regularly to plan strategies for undermining the Constitution, destroying American institutions, rejecting our traditions, overturning duly elected governments, and championing the globalist New World Order. Their nefarious activities impact the freedom and happiness of the entire world.

These organizations are financed by super rich billionaires like the Rockefellers, the Rothchilds, Georges Soros, and Michael Bloomberg. Yes, they are conspirators against America and individual liberty. Hundreds of these organizations exist but three of them seem to have the most impact: The Bilderberger Group, The Council on Foreign Relations, and The Trilateral Commission. Here is my list of these groups:

- Aspen Institute (globalization)
- Atlantic Council (globalization, anti-Trump)
- Bilderberger Group (globalists, worldwide conspirators)

- Bill and Melinda Gates Foundation (vaccines, drugs, population control, Common Core, global warming, funding liberal organizations)
- Bloomberg Family Foundation (global warming, abortion, anti-fossil fuels, gun control)
- Bohemian Grove (elitism, globalism, alleged occult activities)
- Brookings Institution (elitist, leftist, squanders our taxes, ties with many leftist organizations)
- Carnegie Foundation (funds left-wing organizations, pushes socialism)
- Clinton Foundation (uses government positions to enrich the Clintons)
- Club of Rome (global warming alarmism, limits to growth)
- Council on Foreign Relations (globalism)
- Everytown for Gun Safety (anti-gun, funded by Bloomberg)
- Ford Foundation (funds leftist groups, socialism)
- Historical Illuminati
- Le Cercle
- Mayors Against Illegal Guns (anti-gun, funded by Bloomberg)
- Moms Demand Action for Gun Sense (anti-gun, funded by Bloomberg)
- Moveon.org, (funded by conspirator globalist George Soros)
- Open Society Foundations (funded by George Soros, least transparent group in the US)
- Planned Parenthood (abortion clinic funded in part by Michael Bloomberg)
- Rockefeller Brothers Fund
- Rockefeller Family Fund
- Rockefeller Foundation
- Sierra Club (against the coal industry, funded in part by Michael Bloomberg)
- Skull and Bones
- Soros Family Foundation

- Tides Foundation (radical promotion of leftist ideals)
- Trilateral Commission
- World Affairs Council
- World Economic Forum
- World Government Summit
- Young Men's Initiative in partnership with New York City (against ethnic disparities), funded by Bloomberg and Soros)
- Zuckerberg Foundations

WORKS CONSULTED

Alinsky, Saul D. *Rules for Radicals: A Pragmatic Primer for Realistic Radicals*. Vintage Books: New York, 1971.

Angell, Marcia. *The Truth About the Drug Companies: How They Deceive Us and What to Do About It*. Random House: New York, 2004.

Barton, David. *Original Intent: The Courts, the Constitution, and Religion*. WallBuilder Press: Aledo, TX, 1997.

Bastiat, Frederic. *The Law*. The Foundation for Economic Education: New York, 1990.

Bork, Robert H. *The Tempting of America: The Political Seduction of the Law*. Simon & Schuster, Inc.: New York, 1990.

Colter, Ann. *¡Adios America!: The Left's Plan to Turn Our Country into a Third World Hellhole*. Regnery Publishing: Washington, DC, 2015.

Colter, Ann. *How to Talk to A Liberal (If You Must)*. Three Rivers Press: New York, 2005.

Danon, Danny. *Israel Will Prevail*. Palgrave Macmillan: New York, 2013.

Daughtry, Timothy and Casselman, Gary. *Waking the Sleeping Giant*. Beaufort Books: New York, 2012.

DiLorenzo, Thomas J. *The Problem with Socialism*. Regnery Publishing: Washington, DC, 2016.

D'Souza, Dinesh. *The Big Lie: Exposing the Nazi Roots of the American Left*. Regnery Publishing: Washington DC, 2017.

Friedman, Milton. *Capitalism and Freedom*. The University of Chicago Press: Chicago and London, 2002.

The Global Warming Wars, A Documentary Film by South House Entertainment, 2014.

Habakus, Louise Kuo, M.A. and Holland, Mary, editors. *Vaccine Epidemic*. Skyhorse Publishing: New York, 2012.

Herring, Jonathan. *How to Argue Powerfully, Persuasively, Positively*. Pearson Education: Upper Saddle River, NJ, 2012.

Hubbard, Bela. *Political and Economic Structures*. The Caxton Printers, Ltd. Caldwell, Idaho, 1956. (Wikipedia describes Bela Hubbard as a 19th century naturalist, geologist, writer, historian, surveyor, explorer, lawyer, real estate dealer, lumberman and civic leader of early Detroit, Michigan.)

Humphries, Rusty. *7 Ways to Win Political Debates with Your Liberal Family and Friends*. 2017.

Humphries, Suzanne, MD and Bystrianyk, Roman. *Dissolving Illusions*. Humphries and Bystrianyk: np, 2015.

Jackson, Gregory. *Conservative Comebacks to Liberal Lies*. JAJ Publishing: np, 2007.

Kreeft, Peter. *Socratic Logic: A Logic Text Using Socratic Method, Platonic Questions, Aristotelian Principles*, edition 3.1. Saint Augustine's Press: South Bend, IN, 2014.

Liechty, Jay. *America's State Church: Will It Be the Dominant Religion of the 21st Century?* Calder Press: Orem, Utah, 1994.

Loewen, James W. *Lies My Teacher Told Me: Everything Your American History Textbook Got Wrong*. Simon and Schuster: New York, 2007.

Lofgren, John. *Atlas Shouts*. Abbott Press: Bloomington, IN, 2014.

Lott, John, Jr. *More Guns, Less Crime: Understanding Crime and Gun-Control Laws*, Third Edition. The University of Chicago Press: Chicago, 2010.

Lott, John, Jr. *War on Guns: Arming Yourself Against Gun-Control Lies*. Regnery Press: Washington, DC, 2016.

Martin, Michael G. *Liberalism: The Demise of America*. Sophistopia Press: 2013.

Mgrdechian, Richard. *How the Left Was Won*. Coventry Circle: San Francisco, 2006.

Miller, Neil Z. *Miller's Review of Critical Vaccine Studies: 400 Important Scientific Papers Summarized for Parents and Researchers*. New Atlantean Press: Santa Fe, New Mexico, 2016.

Morano, Marc. *The Politically Incorrect Guide to Climate Change*. Regnery Publishing: Washington D.C., 2018.

Newton, Michael E. *The Path to Tyranny: A History of Free Society's Descent Into Tyranny*, second edition. Eleftheria Publishing: USA, 2010.

Ostrowski, James. *Progressivism: A Primer on the Idea Destroying America*. Cazenovia Books: Buffalo, NY, 2014.

Paul, Rand. *Government Bullies: How Everyday Americans Are Being Harassed, Abused, and Imprisoned by the Feds*. Center Street: New York, 2012.

Reed, Lawrence W. *Excuse Me, Professor: Challenging the Myths of Progressivism*. Regnery Publishing: Washington, DC, 2015.

Roberts, Paul Craig and Stratton, Lawrence M. *The Tyranny of Good Intentions: How Prosecutors and Bureaucrats Are Trampling the Constitution in the Name of Justice*. Forum: Roseville, CA, 2000.

Rossiter, Lyle H., Jr. *The Liberal Mind: The Psychological Causes of Political Madness*. Free World Books, LLC: St. Charles, IL, 2008.

Rottenberg, Annette T. *Elements of Argument: A Text and a Reader*, third edition. Bedford Books of St. Martin's Press: Boston, 1991.

Shapiro, Ben. *Bullies: How the Left's Culture of Fear and Intimidation Silences Americans*. Threshold Editions: New York, 2013.

Skousen, W. Cleon. *The Making of America: The Substance and Meaning of the Constitution*, third edition. The National Center for Constitutional Studies: Malta, ID, 2007.

Spencer, Robert. *The Truth About Muhammad, Founder of the World's Most Intolerant Religion*. Regnery Publishing: Washington, DC, 2006.

Stormer, John A. *Betrayed by the Bench: How Judge-Made Law Has Transformed America's Constitution, Courts and Culture*. Liberty Bell Press: Florissant, Missouri, 2005.

Taylor, Kathleen. *Brainwashing: The Science of Thought Control*. Oxford University Press: 2004.

Tenpenny, Sherri, Dr. *Saying No to Vaccines: A Resource Guide for All Ages*. Tenpenny Vaccine Info.: Cleveland, OH, 2008.

Valentine, Phil. *The Conservative's Handbook*. Cumberland House: Naperville, IL., 2008.

Weston, Anthony. *A Rulebook for Arguments*, fifth edition. Hackett Publishing: Indianapolis, 2017.

Woods, Thomas E., Jr. *The Politically Incorrect Guide to American History*. Regnery Publishing, Inc.: Washington, DC, 2004.

Zmirak, John and Perrotta, Al. *The Politically Incorrect Guide to Immigration: An America First Manifesto*. Regnery Publishing: Washington, DC, 2018.

About the Author

After observing and studying the American social and political scenes all his adult life, Kenneth R. Tarr has been astounded at the long history of anti-American lies sold to America and the world by left-wing pundits and politicians, including liberals and progressives, who spread their lies through an endless litany of deceptive strategies. He has also engaged in thousands of debates with these people, and those debates have taught him a great deal about exposing and defeating their duplicitous tactics. He has shared this vital information in his book *Defeating Liberal Lies.*

Kenneth earned a PhD in his chosen field and this has provided him with the expertise to do research and accurately analyze and evaluate sources and arguments. He has written a total of ten books and in most of these books he has striven to oppose everything leftists stand for.

Kenneth is a proud constitutional conservative who is determined to defend America against the evils of liberalism, socialism, and Communism propagated by people who will do anything to destroy America in order to gain wealth and power.

Kenneth has written six novels for adults, a youth novel, and two non-fiction books. He welcomes questions and comments. Address them to kennethtarr@ranunes.com.

Made in the USA
Middletown, DE
08 February 2021